the cart,
No one hates the simple little bastard
Like a newspaper can. (*Long sustained chord*)
(*House Tabs in*)

(*The End*)

A Garland Series

RENAISSANCE DRAMA

A COLLECTION OF
CRITICAL EDITIONS

edited by
STEPHEN ORGEL
The Johns Hopkins University

THE TROUBLESOME RAIGNE OF JOHN, KING OF ENGLAND

J.W. SIDER

GARLAND PUBLISHING, INC.
NEW YORK & LONDON · 1979

All volumes in this series are printed on
acid-free, 250-year-life paper.

Library of Congress Cataloging in Publication Data

Troublesome raigne of John, King of England.
  The troublesome raigne of John, King of England.

  (Renaissance drama)
  Includes bibliographical references and index.
  1. John, King of England, 1167?– 1216 —Drama.
I. Sider, J. W., 1941 –   II. Series.
PR2411.T75   1979   822'.3   78-66778
ISBN 0-8240-9733-5

CONTENTS

ACKNOWLEDGMENTS

This dissertation was submitted in June 1970 in partial fulfillment
of the requirements for the Ph.D. degree at the University of Notre Dame.
For able and friendly supervision I thank my director, Professor Robert
J. Lordi, and the readers, Professors Walter R. Davis, Paul E. McLane,
and Paul A. Rathburn. Section V of the introduction was not a part of
the original dissertation.

I am indebted to the authorities of the Folger Shakespeare Library
and the Huntington Library, and to the Master and Fellows of Trinity
College Cambridge, for permission to make use of their copies of the
first edition of The Troublesome Raigne; for this I express thanks, and
also for the cooperation of the Newberry Library and the University of
Illinois Library. The Curators of the Bodleian Library kindly granted
permission for the reproduction of the "Declaration" of Sixtus V.

The Canada Council granted me a fellowship which was an indispens-
able contribution.

I am grateful to Mr. Palmer Cone and Mrs. Patricia Slocum of the
Memorial Library, University of Notre Dame, for many courtesies; and to
Professor George R. Price of Michigan State University, Dr. Bruce Brown,
my sister Miriam Scott, and my son Philip, who assisted me in various
ways.

My chief debt, first and last, is to my wife, Anna.

ABBREVIATIONS

For editions of the Raigne mentioned by abbreviation only in the textual notes, see the introduction to the text, section 2.

Arber   A Transcript of the Registers of the Company of Stationers of London; 1554-1640 A.D., ed. Edward Arber. 5 vols. London, 1875-1894.

Bullough   Narrative and Dramatic Sources of Shakespeare, IV, ed. Geoffrey Bullough. London: Routledge & Kegan Paul; New York: Columbia University Press, 1962.

Chambers   E. K. Chambers, William Shakespeare: A Study of Facts and Problems. 2 vols. Oxford: Clarendon Press, 1951.

Dominic   "The Troublesome Reign of King John: A Critical Edition," ed. Joseph Francis Dominic. Unpublished Ph.D. dissertation, Michigan State University, 1969.

Foxe   John Foxe, Actes and Monuments, 1583.

Gary   Suzanne Tumblin Gary, "The Relationship between The Troublesome Reign of John King of England and Shakespeare's King John." Unpublished Ph.D. dissertation, University of Arizona, 1971.

Halliwell   James Orchard Halliwell-Phillipps, A Dictionary of Archaic and Provincial Words, 6th ed. 2 vols. London: John Russell Smith, 1868-1872.

Holinshed   Raphael Holinshed, Chronicles, 2nd ed. 1587.

Honigmann   William Shakespeare, King John, ed. E. A. J. Honigmann (New Arden) London: Methuen; Cambridge, Mass.: Harvard University Press, 1954. Quotations from King John are cited from this edition.

Hopkinson   The Troublesome Reign of King John, ed. A. F. Hopkinson. London: M. E. Sims & Co., 1896.

Munro   'The Troublesome Reign of King John' . . . , ed. F. J. Furnivall and John Munro. New York: Duffield & Co; London: Chatto & Windus, 1913.

OED   The Oxford English Dictionary

Paris   Matthew Paris, Chronica Majora, ed. Henry Richards Luard. 7 vols. London: Longman, 1874.

PMLA   Publications of the Modern Language Association of America

Tilley   Morris Palmer Tilley, A Dictionary of the Proverbs in England in the Sixteenth and Seventeenth Centuries. Ann Arbor: University of Michigan Press, 1950.

TLS   (London) Times Literary Supplement

Wilson   William Shakespeare, King John, ed. John Dover Wilson (New Cambridge). Cambridge: Cambridge University Press, 1954.

INTRODUCTION

I   THE TEXT

1. The First Edition

The first known edition of The Troublesome Raigne was published in
1591 in two quarto volumes. Though none of the three extant copies[1] is
perfect, one supplies what is missing in another, so that the ideal copy
can be described as follows.

Part I

<THE> | Troublesome Raigne | of Iohn King of England, with the dis- |
couerie of King Richard Cordelions | Base sonne (vulgarly named, The Ba- |
stard Fawconbridge): also the | death of King Iohn at Swinstead | Abbey. |
As it was (sundry times) publikely acted by the | Queenes Maiesties
Players, in the ho- | nourable Citie of | London. | [device] | Imprinted
at London for Sampson Clarke, | and are to be solde at his shop, on the
backe- | side of the Royall Exchange. | 1591.

HT] [ornament] | The troublesome Raigne of | King Iohn.

RT] The troublesome Raigne | of King Iohn.

Collation: 4°: A-G⁴, 28 leaves unnumbered.

A1: joint title (verso blank). A2: preface "To the Gentlemen Readers." (11 lines) (verso blank). A3: text with HT and initial. On
G4^v: "The ende of the first part."

Catchwords: A4^v And   B2 Was [Robert Was]   B3^v Slaun- [Slaunder]   C4

Ba- [Bastard]   D4^v And   E1 stolike [stolick]   E1^v Con- [Confusion]

E2 Con- [Constance]   F4^v (Simplie [(Simply]   G2 Confir- [Confirming]

Copies: Capell (head cropped)   Folger (lacking A1)   Huntington (lacking
A1)

---

[1] In the Capell Collection at Trinity College, Cambridge; in the Folger
Shakespeare Library; and in the Huntington Library. Hereafter the copies
are designated as "Capell," "Folger," and "Huntington."

Part II

〈THE〉 | Second part of the | troublesome Raigne of King | Iohn, conteining
the death | of Arthur Plantaginet, | the landing of Lewes, and | the
poysning of King | Iohn at Swinstead | Abbey. | As it was (sundry times)
publikely acted by the | Queenes Maiesties Players, in the ho- |
nourable Citie of | London. | [ornament] | Imprinted at London for Sampson
Clarke, | and are to be solde at his shop, on the backe- | side of the
Royall Exchange. | 1591.

HT] [ornament] | The second part of the troublesome Raigne | of King
Iohn, containing the entraunce of Lewes | the French Kings sonne: with the
poysoning of King | Iohn by a Monke.

RT] The troublesome Raigne | of King Iohn.

Collation: 4°: A-E^4, 20 leaves unnumbered.

A1: title (verso blank). A2: preface "To the Gentlmen Readers." (15
lines) (verso blank). A3: text with HT and initial. On E4^V: "FINIS."

Catchwords: A4^V The   B4^V If   C3 Thomas [I Thomas]   C4 Enter [Enter]

D4 Monk My

Copies: Capell (head cropped)   Folger (lacking E2-4)   Huntington

Notes to both parts:

1. The bulk of the text and most of the signatures are set in black letter;
a few specifically designated words in the text, the running titles, and
the stage directions (generally, except proper names) are set in roman
type; the prefaces, the speech heads, and proper names (generally) are set
in italic type.

2. The cropping in Capell has removed almost all of the first word on each
title page, most or all of every running title, and in a few cases part of
the first line of the text.

3. The device on the title page of Part I is numbered 273ϗ by R. B. McKer-

row. His description follows: "(43 × 39 mm.) Framed device of clasped

hands emerging from clouds, holding a caduceus and two cornucopias, with

T. O. below the hands. The motto, By wisdom peace. By peace plenty."[2]

4. One irregularity in the running titles appears in Part I, C3^v: "The

Troublesome Raiəu̇ꝫ."

5. I have seen Capell and Folger only in mechanical copies.

According to the title page the two parts of Q1 were "imprinted at

London for Sampson Clarke," bookseller. To McKerrow's account of him I

have nothing to add:

This stationer was made free of the Company on March 26th, 1583, by
George Buck and William Broome [Arber, ii. 687]. His first book entry
was made on November 4th, 1583, and related to Thomas Lodge's Tryed
experiences of worldlie abuses (i.e., An Alarm against Usurers) [Arber,
ii. 428]. He also dealt in ballads. Sampson Clarke was one of the de-
fendants in the suit brought in 1585 by the assigns of Richard Day against
certain stationers for unlawfully printing and selling The A B C and Li-
tell Catechisme [Arber, ii. 791, 792]. He was admitted to the livery on
July 1st, 1598 [Arber, ii. 873].[3]

The ornament on the title page of Part I is found in books produced

by a London printer, Thomas Orwin, and by his widow.[4] This is our only

link between play and printer, since there is no entry for the play in

the Stationers' Register. Orwin finished his apprenticeship under Thomas

Purfoote on May 5, 1581 (Arber, II, 684). When the printer George Robin-

son died (c. 1586),[5] Orwin married his widow and acquired the business.

His first entry in the Stationers' Register was on July 1, 1588, and his

last on May 7, 1593 (Arber, II, 493, 630). An entry on June 25, 1593

[2] Printers' & Publishers' Devices in England & Scotland 1485-1640 (London:
The Bibliographical Society, 1949), p. 105.

[3] A Dictionary of Printers and Booksellers, ed. R. B. McKerrow (London: The
Bibliographical Society, 1910), p. 70.

[4] McKerrow, Printers' and Publishers' Devices, p. 105.

[5] McKerrow, Dictionary of Printers, p. 230.

(Arber, II, 186), indicates that he was by then deceased. Other entries involve political polemic, including a ballade of the strange whippes whiche the Spanyardes had prepared [for] the Englishemen and women (1588), and a ballad called a Trewe Saylers songe against Spanyshe pride (Arber, II, 498, 542). But Martin Marprelate charges that he "sometimes wrought popish bookes in corners: namely Iesus Psalter our Ladies Psalter &c."[6] And Thomas Cooper, Bishop of Winchester, replied that "Thomas Orwin himselfe hath upon his booke oath denied, that he ever printed, either Iesus Psalter, or Our Lady Psalter, or that hee ever was any worker about them, or about any the like bookes."[7] Perhaps Orwin had only one press in 1591: two entries in the Stationers' Register (Arber, I, 555; V, li) refer to his "press" in the singular. Ordinary impreciseness of language might easily account for one instance, but less likely for the coincidence of two.

There is no clear evidence in Part I of more than one compositor, but the consistency of his spelling habits makes it unlikely that he did any work on Part II, where spelling variants (as well as a few omitted speech heads and some lines of verse printed as prose) have been thought to suggest more than one compositor,[8] but are more likely the work of one inconsistent speller since there is no clear pattern corresponding to ordinary composing stints. Q1 was set by formes, if we may assume no major interruption of the work between sheets; for type from one sheet frequently appears in the first pages of the next. Copy set by formes must be cast off, and Q1 shows some evidences of this process. Dominic (p. 134) infers

[6]Epistle, ed. Edward Arber, The English Scholar's Library of Old and Modern Works, 11 (London, 1880), p. 23.

[7]An Admonition to the People of England (London: Deputies of Christopher Barker, 1589), p. 43.

[8]Dominic, pp. 142-146.

from the thirty-six-line page format that the printer planned from the beginning thus to accommodate the whole play in twelve sheets; he notes also inconsistencies in the use of blank lines to set off stage directions within scenes--presumably a sign of adjusting copy to the space assigned. Nearly half the pages of the play show other signs of crowding such as the ampersand,[9] tilde,[10] and /y/ for /th/[11]--always avoiding a new line. With the same evident purpose there are ends of lines bracketed to the line above or below,[12] abbreviated spellings in speeches,[13] and many speech heads which are indented only partially, or not at all.[14] Some of the pages thus crowded also have stage directions set off by blank lines, possibly because the printers tried not to alter an original plan of spacing the directions.

The running titles of Q1 recur as indicated in Figure 1. A full complement for one forme consists of two complete titles--four halves. There are four settings in Q1 of the first half ("The Troublesome Raigne"), numbered I, III, V, and VII in Figure 1; and four settings of the second half ("of King Iohn."), numbered II, IV, VI, and VIII. The two sheets A are identical in layout; and some of their corresponding pages contain identical types and ornaments in the same positions, as follows: 1^r--the types on the lower half, from "As it was (sundry times)" to the end; 2^r--the ornament above the preface; 3^r--the ornament above the head-title; 3^v, 4^r, 4^v--the running titles. The two parts are not, then, "bibliographically

[9]IA4, S.D.; IB1, 7; IC2, S.D.; $IC2^v$, 36; etc.

[10]$IC2^v$, 34; $IF1^v$, 24; $IIB1^v$, 17; etc.

[11]$IF1^v$, 30; $IIC4^v$, 16; IIE2, 18; etc.

[12]$IF1^v$, 26; $IG1^v$, 7; $IIB4^v$, 14; etc.

[13]$IE2^v$, 7, 14.

[14]$IIA3^v$, 32; IIA4, 25; IIC3, 5; etc.

Figure 1: Running Titles of Q1

Part I--Sheets B to G

IV	III		IV	III
2	3^V		1	4^V
I	II		I	II
1^V	4		2^V	3

inner   outer

Parts I, II--Sheet A   Part II--Sheets B, D

PREFACE	III		TITLE PAGE	III
2	3^V		1	4^V
BLANK	VI		BLANK	HEAD-TITLE
1^V	4		2^V	3

inner   outer

IV	V		IV	V
2	3^V		1	4^V
I	II		I	II
1^V	4		2^V	3

inner   outer

Part II--Sheet C   Part II--Sheet E

VIII	III		VIII	III
4	1^V		3	2^V
VII	VI		VII	VI
3^V	2		4^V	1

inner   outer

VIII	III		VIII	III
2	3^V		1	4^V
VII	VI		VII	VI
1^V	4		2^V	3

inner   outer

independent,"[15] except in that Part II begins with a new sheet A. The
hypothesis which seems best suited to these facts follows. Sheets B to G
of Part I were set up by compositor A and impressed in alphabetical order,
each outer forme succeeding each inner forme in a single skeleton. Compositor A then set up the outer forme of sheet IA and compositor B set up
the outer forme of sheet IIA; while these two formes were being impressed
(with only one of the four half titles used for Part I), compositor B was
using the other three half titles, with a newly composed replacement for
the fourth, for his composition of the inner forme of sheet IIB in a second
skeleton. Meanwhile compositor A set up the inner forme of sheet IA; it
was impressed in the first skeleton after the outer formes of the two
sheets A were completed. But since the inner forme required two halves of
running titles (to the outer forme's one), and since the other running
titles were already set up in a second skeleton with the inner forme of
IIB, compositor A set up one more element to restore a half-complement of
running titles to the first skeleton for the inner formes of the sheets A.
After seeing the inner forme of sheet IIB into the press, compositor B set
up the inner forme of IIA; and then he set up in succession the outer
forme of sheet IIB and the inner and outer formes of IIC, IID, and IIE--
using the second skeleton for both formes of sheets B and D, and the first
(with two more newly-set half titles) for both formes of sheets C and E.
It is not clear why the two sets of running titles (and two skeletons,
presumably) used in Part II should alternate not by forme but by sheet.

These are the press variants which I have found in Q1:

IB2, 27 (i.230). thy] Capell, Huntington; thy thy Folger.

IB2^V, 9 (i.248). proeede] Capell, Huntington; proeeede Folger.

---

[15] W. W. Greg, A Bibliography of the English Printed Drama to the Restora-
tion, 4 vols. (London: The Bibliographical Society, 1939-1959), I, 178.

IB2^V, 36 (1.275). cannot] <u>Capell, Huntington;</u> cann ot <u>Folger</u>.

IB3, 10 (i.285). hath] <u>Capell, Huntington;</u> ha h <u>Folger</u>.

IB3^V, 24 (i.336). slaunder] <u>Capell, Huntington;</u> fiaunder <u>Folger</u>.

IG1^V, 4 (viii.61). eccho] <u>Folger, Huntington;</u> etcho <u>Capell</u>.

IIC3, 3 (xi. 188). requite] <u>Folger, Huntington;</u> rêquite <u>Capell</u>.

IIC3^V, 31 (xi.251). Ile] <u>Folger, Huntington;</u> Il <u>Capell</u>.

An intelligent reader might make the extant press corrections without referring to the copy. Some readings of Q1 make no sense at all, and sense or rhyme sometimes suggest that something has been omitted.[16] If the proof-reader were the author, or the printer checking against his copy, some of these errors would hardly have been overlooked.

The quarto of 1591 was probably printed from foul papers or an author-ial fair copy; the alternatives all seem less likely. Dominic's three ear-marks of printed copy (pp. 132-135) are not significant: since the discovery of casting off copy, the inclusion of text in the first sheet is meaning-less; the minimal press corrections may suggest good copy, but not neces-sarily printed copy; and the printers' regular page-format reflects casting off more likely than printed copy. Indeed, the frequent crowding more plausibly suggests the inexact estimates of casting off a manuscript, than the accurate predictions made possible by printed copy; in this respect the differences between Q1 and Q2 are instructive.

Should the <u>Raigne</u> prove to be a special kind of piracy of Shakespeare's <u>King John</u>, as some have suggested, the play might have been written for publication only. If the play were not actable by an Elizabethan company, the copytext could not be a prompt-copy. But the <u>Raigne</u>'s forty-odd speaking parts can be executed in the manner customary to a company of

[16]E.g. i.307, vi.76, xi.53-55.

twelve men and four boys (with stage hands for mute roles).[17] Such a cast

is the minimum indicated by the number of speaking characters at Angiers;

and the play is especially trimmed for this cast in the stage direction

at xv.125.1-2 and in the two ensuing scenes, where Salisbury is the only

baron mentioned directly. The poisoning scene requires two friars to lay

the cloth, Monk Thomas and the Abbot, John and the Bastard, Pandulph and

Salisbury, and two messengers—ten men; and Lewis is waiting to begin the

next scene. I know of no way of reassigning parts to make the one remain-

ing man (number 10 in the suggested scheme) Pembroke or Essex; apparently

"the Barons" of the stage direction consisted of this man, the available

supernumeraries, and Salisbury. Evidently the Raigne was written to be

acted, though no evidence of a stage history exists beyond the mention of

the Queen's Players on the title pages. Yet Wilfred T. Jewkes finds "no

indication that [the Q1 text] may have been prepared for the stage,"[18]

and the evidence following here virtually eliminates prompt-copy as the

possible provenance. R. B. McKerrow suggests that the few plays which had

[17]Men   1   John
          2   Bastard
          3   Robert, Pandulph, Hubert's 1st Attendant
          4   Salisbury
          5   Pembroke, Friar Thomas, 1st Friar of Swinstead
          6   Citizen, Hubert, Beauchamp, Monk Thomas
          7   Philip of France, Percy, Abbot
          8   Sheriff, Lewis, Hubert's 2nd Attendant
          9   Essex, Limoges, 1st French Messenger, Friar Anthony, 2nd Friar
              of Swinstead
         10   Chattilion, Hubert's 3rd Attendant, Melun
         11   English Herald, Friar Laurence, French Lord, 2nd French Messen-
              ger, Messenger (last scene)
         12   French Herald, Peter, 3rd French Messenger, Messenger (last
              scene)
    Boys 1   Elinor, Boy with Peter
          2   Margaret (Lady Falconbridge), Blanch
          3   Arthur, Henry
          4   Constance, Alice the Nun

[18]Act Division in Elizabethan and Jacobean Plays, 1593-1616 (Hamden, Conn.:
Shoe-String Press, 1958), p. 200.

such provenance[19] are unmistakable because of the specific and rigorous

demands made of prompt-copy (pp. 270-272). The _Raigne_ entirely lacks

three of McKerrow's earmarks: advance warnings for actors or properties;

mention at an actor's entrance of properties not to be used or displayed

until later; and the addition of an actor's name to that of the character

whom he represents. And there is but one uncertain case of McKerrow's

fourth earmark.[20] Further, features are missing from the _Raigne_ which

are essential to prompt-copy, though not peculiar to it. Prompt-copy

could not omit entrances and exits as Q1 does, and since that text is

reasonably competent in other respects we can hardly accuse the printer.

Dominic offers evidence for a non-authorial transcript of foul pa-

pers, but his examples of scribal mishearings (_Shattilion_ for _Chattilion_,

Hughbert for _Hubert_, _Nidigate_ for _Newdigate_, _was_ for _wakes_, and _tree_ for

three) are attributable to other causes, and he admits that his supposed

instances of interpolation due to dictation could be the author's work.[21]

The remaining evidence admits the possibility of either foul papers or

authorial fair copy. Omitted speech heads, entrances, and exits are

generally taken as signs of foul papers. These earmarks themselves make

fairly adequate proof--as good as we are likely to find, for various other

indicators readily admit alternate explanations: permissive stage direc-

tions, mislineations, directions introducing characters to scenes where

they have nothing to do.

Q1 does intimate other things about the copytext. First, because the

---

[19]"The Elizabethan Printer and Dramatic Manuscripts," _The Library_, 4th ser.,
XII (1931-32), 268.

[20]Constance's premature entrance (v.0.2) may be a prompt-copy's anticipa-
tory warning to the actor; but the author could have decided, after writing
it, to keep her off stage during King Philip's callous unconcern about the
capture of Arthur.

[21]Dominic, pp. 68-70, 128.

printed text displays a few obvious corrections but not many, the copytext was probably not much corrupted. Complete clarity might suggest
that the proofreader carefully made some sense of everything; but sprink-
led obscurities give some assurance that we have the copytext with little
alteration. Second, the widely varying spellings of Q1 cannot reflect
clearly the work of more than one author, if this text was set by two
compositors. Third, we may gather that the copytext was not divided,
since Part I resolves nothing and the beginning of Part II is obscure by
itself. Perhaps the publisher wished to charge buyers double on the precedent of Marlowe's Tamburlaine, a play mentioned in the preface and
first published the previous year in two legitimate parts with an address
"To the Gentlemen Readers." Honigmann says: "Both the title-page and
lines 'To the Gentlemen Readers' of Part I promise the death of John,
which takes place in Part II. Such overlapping can be paralleled c. 1590
in two-part learned works with separate title-pages and signatures, but
seems suspicious in plays" (pp. 175-176).

2. Later Editions

        Except for two mechanical reproductions, no edition since Q2 has been
based entirely on the first.

> THE | First and second Part of | the troublesome Raigne of | John
> King of England. | With the discoverie of King Richard Cor- | delions
> Base sonne (vulgarly named, The Bastard | Fawconbridge:) Also, the
> death of King John | at Swinstead Abbey. | As they were (sundry times)
> lately acted by | the Queenes Majesties Players. | Written by W. Sh. |
> [ornament] | Imprinted at London by Valentine Simmes for John Helme, |
> and are to be sold at his shop in Saint Dunstons|Churchyard in
> Fleetestreet. | 1611.

Q2 is a reprint in one volume of the two parts of Q1, in roman type with
some italic for speech heads, etc. The date and ascription to "W. Sh."
may indicate that the publisher intended to deceive unwary buyers looking

for Shakespeare's <u>King</u> <u>John</u> (apparently unpublished till 1623); the sup-
pression of the phrase "in the honourable city of London" from the title
page of Q1 makes some kind of deception likely. This edition corrects
some obvious misprints of Q1, but introduces many new errors. Almost all
of the editions before 1900 are based wholly or partly on Q2 or its heirs.

> THE | First and second Part of | the troublesome Raigne of | John
> King of England. | <u>With</u> <u>the</u> <u>discoverie</u> <u>of</u> <u>King</u> Richard Cor- | delions
> Base sonne (vulgarly named, the Bastard | <u>Fauconbridge</u>:) Also the
> death of King | <u>John</u> at Swinstead Abbey. | As they were (<u>sundry</u> <u>times</u>)
> <u>lately</u> <u>acted.</u> ‖ Written by W. Shakespeare. ‖ [device] | London, |
> Printed by <u>Aug</u>: <u>Mathewes</u> for <u>Thomas</u> <u>Dewe</u>, and are to⌊be sold at his
> shop in St. Dunstones Church⁓ | yard in Fleet-street, 1622.

Q3 is a reprint of Q2. The bolder ascription to "W. Shakespeare" may anti-
cipate the first known printing of his <u>John</u> in the Folio of 1623: its publication was announced well in advance, and some plays of Shakespeare
appeared in competing quartos before the collection appeared. Q3 makes
sophisticated emendations, but they have not been much reproduced as no
subsequent editor except Dominic appears to have consulted Q3.

> Miscellaneous Pieces of Antient English Poesie. Viz. The Troublesome
> Raigne of King John, Written by Shakespeare, Extant in no Edition of
> his Writings. The Metamorphosis of Pigmalion's Image, and certain
> Satyres. By John Marston. The Scourge of Villanie. By the same.
> All printed before the Year 1600. London: Printed for Robert Horse-
> field, at the Crown in Ludgate-Street. M.DCC.LXIV.

John Bowle's edition, pp. 1-113, is an old-spelling reprint of Q2 with a
brief introduction.

> Twenty of the Plays of Shakespeare, Being the whole Number printed
> in Quarto During his Life-time, or before the Restoration, Collated
> where there were different Copies, and Publish'd from the Originals,
> By George Steevens, Esq; In Four Volumes. . . . London: Printed for
> J. and R. Tonson, in the Strand; T. Payne, at the Mews-gate,
> Castle-street; and W. Richardson, in Fleet-street. M.DCC.LXVI.

Steevens' edition, II, N7-T7^v, is an old-spelling reprint of Q2 with a
general introduction in volume I and a brief introduction to the <u>Raigne</u>.

Six Old Plays, on which Shakspeare Founded His Measure for Measure.
Comedy of Errors. Taming the Shrew. King John. K. Henry IV. and K.
Henry V. King Lear. In Two Volumes. . . . London, Printed for S.
Leacroft, Charing-Cross: And sold by J. Nichols, Red-Lion Passage,
Fleet-street; T. Evans, in the Strand; and H. Payne, Pall Mall.
MDCCLXXIX.

John Nichols' edition, II, 217-315, is an old-spelling reprint of Stee-

vens without apparatus.

Alt-Englisches Theater. Oder Supplemente zum Shakspear. Übersezt
und herausgegeben von Ludwig Tieck. [2 vols.] . . . Berlin, in der
Realschulbuchhandlung. 1811.

Tieck's edition, I, 1-157, is a verse-translation into German--the only

translation I have found. A general introduction identifies Shakespeare

as author. Of the editions I have seen, this alone divides the whole play

into five acts.

Shakespeare's Library: A Collection of the Plays Romances Novels
Poems and Histories Employed by Shakespeare in the Composition of
His Works with Introductions and Notes . . . The Text now First
formed from a New Collation of the Original Copies. London: Reeves
and Turner, 1875.

William Carey Hazlitt's edition, V, 221-320, is old-spelling; it is evi-

dently based on a copy of Nichols sporadically corrected from Q1. An

introduction is the only apparatus.

The Life and Death of King John. By William Shakespeare. Together
with the Troublesome Reign of King John, As Acted by the Queen's
players, c. 1589. London and Glasgow: Collins, 1878.

Frederick Gard Fleay's edition, pp. 127-204, the first in modern spelling,

is apparently based on Hazlitt (cited as "Q1") with some corrections from

Q2. There is an introduction, and notes textual and explanatory.

The Life and Death of King John, by Wm. Shakespeare. Cassell's National Library, Vol. II, No. 96. New York: Cassell & Company, 1887.

Henry Morley's edition, pp. 141-192, is a singularly uncritical reprint

of Hazlitt without apparatus. Substantial passages are omitted (evidently

to accommodate the publisher's format); most are summarized in prose.

The Troublesome Raigne of John, King of England. The First Quarto, 1591, which Shakspere rewrote (about 1595) as his "Life and Death of King John." Parts I and II, 2 vols. London: C. Praetorius, 1888.

This is a photolithographic facsimile of the Capell copy of Q1. Because it has been retouched throughout it is inaccurate in some substantive and many accidental readings. Part I reprints Edward Rose's "Shakespeare as an Adapter" from Macmillan's Magazine, November 1878, pp. 69-77, and Part II contains excerpts from Holinshed with remarks by F. J. Furnivall on "The old Playwright's treatment of his Material."

The Life and Death of King John (The Players' Text of The Troublesome Raigne, &c., of 1591, with the Heminges and Condell Text of the King John of 1623). The Bankside Shakespeare, XVIII. New York: The Shakespeare Society of New York, 1892.

This is a type facsimile by Appleton Morgan of the Raigne (derived from Praetorius' facsimile) and Shakespeare's King John, F1, with introduction. The text of the Raigne contains Praetorius' variants and new ones.

The Troublesome Reign of King John. London: M. E. Sims & Co., 1896.

This is a modern-spelling edition by A. F. Hopkinson based on Hazlitt with corrections (probably) from Q2. Apparatus includes a critical and historical introduction, and explanatory and textual notes. Of the editions I have seen, this alone divides each part of the play into five acts. According to the Catalog of Books Represented by Library of Congress Printed Cards[22] the imprint is fictitious.

The Troublesome Reign of John, King of England . . . 1591, ed. John S. Farmer. 2 vols. The Tudor Facsimile Texts. [London?] Issued for Subscribers by the Editor of the Tudor Facsimile Texts, 1911.

This is a clear and unretouched photographic facsimile of the Capell copy of Q1, with a brief introduction.

[22]167 vols. (Ann Arbor, Mich.: Edwards Brothers, (1942-1946), LXX, 149.

'The Troublesome Reign of King John': Being the Original of Shake-
speare's 'Life and Death of King John', ed. F. J. Furnivall and John
Munro. The Shakespeare Classics, I. Gollancz, general editor. New
York: Duffield & Company; London: Chatto & Windus, 1913.

This is a modern-spelling edition based on Praetorius, with extensive

introduction, time scheme, key to correspondences with Shakespeare, and

textual notes. Furnivall died in 1910; a first fragment of the introduc-

tion is the only part of this edition, in its final form, for which he

was responsible.

The Life and Death of King John. A New Variorum Edition of Shakespeare. Philadelphia and London: J. B. Lippincott, 1919.

Horace Howard Furness, Jr. based this modern-spelling edition (pp. 471-

537) on a copy of Munro with corrections from Q1. He included a collec-

tion of critical comments, pp. 447-470.

Narrative and Dramatic Sources of Shakespeare, IV. London: Routledge and Kegan Paul; New York: Columbia University Press, 1962.

Geoffrey Bullough's old-spelling edition (pp. 72-151) is based on Prae-

torius with a few emendations and numerous substantive and accidental

variants. The apparatus includes an introduction to the Raigne and other

sources of King John, notes on parallels with Shakespeare, and explana-

tory notes. The volume also contains excerpts from Bale and Holinshed

pertaining both to the Raigne and to King John.

Six Early Plays Related to the Shakespeare Canon (Anglistica, XIV).
Copenhagen: Rosenkilde and Bagger, 1965.

E. B. Everitt's modern-spelling edition (pp. 143-193), based on Q1 and

Furness, includes a brief critical introduction, a note on the text, and

a list of emendations.

The Troublesome Reign of King John: A Critical Edition. Unpublished
Ph.D. dissertation, Michigan State University, 1969.

Joseph Francis Dominic's edition is the first to represent a collation of

the three known copies of Q1. Textual notes record about half the substantive and semi-substantive variants of Q2 and Q3, some of the editor's emendations, and a few emendations from Fleay, Munro, and Bullough.[23] An introduction discusses authorship and sources, the provenance of Q1, the tradition of the history play, the evidence that Q1 is not an ordinary bad quarto of Shakespeare's <u>King John</u>, and several later editions.

All of these texts, except Tieck and Farmer, have been collated for this text.

3. This Edition

The present edition is based on a collation of the three known copies of Q1. Textual notes on press variants give the altered reading first, then the original reading. Some variants seem deliberate; some may be due to accidentally shifted types.

Because Q1 is the only authoritative text there is no way of distinguishing the author's accidentals from the compositors'; hence in general this edition preserves the accidentals of the copytext. Except for the regular silent alterations mentioned below, all emendations of the copytext are recorded in the textual notes. The reading of this edition is followed by a square bracket and the siglum of the earliest edition in which the adopted reading appears; last is the reading of Q1. Accidental variations between an adopted reading and the first edition in which it appears are not recorded. Emendations without sigla in the textual notes originate with this edition. Where significant emendations have been rejected all of the emending editions are noted, and the adopted reading is

[23] Many of Bullough's variants recur here unnoted; perhaps the copytext was Bullough incompletely corrected from Q1. Dominic knows of only seven editions after the quartos: none is fully collated except Bullough, and three of them he shows no sign of having seen.

defended in the explanatory notes. Editorical additions conform to the normal accidentals of Q1.

Several passages of false prose have been changed to verse, with suitable capitals added silently. Hypermetrics have been relined where they consist of two iambic pentameter lines or of one iambic pentameter line and an extrametrical exclamation. The punctuation of Q1 is generally light and sometimes at odds with modern conventions; in the few passages which might confuse the modern reader the punctuation is emended and the change noted. Asides are not explicitly marked in Q1; where the sense requires an aside or a shift of address, this edition adds or substitutes dashes; there are no dashes in Q1.

Here is a list of other silent alterations. Full stops are supplied where they are missing at the ends of speeches, except for the few interrupted speeches where a dash is added. Spaces and margins are regularized; the letters /j/, /v/, /u/, long /s/, and the black-letter long /r/ are made to conform to modern usage; thorns, tildes, ampersands, and arabic numerals are expanded, ligatures ignored, and letters in the wrong font corrected. Single turned letters are restored silently where they create no new word. Catchwords are omitted, and signatures are supplied opposite the first line of each page of Q1. Ornaments are omitted; ornamental letters and the capitals following them are altered silently. Each speech head is regularized and set on the line preceding the speech.

In reducing three fonts of type to two it has been possible to preserve the deliberate contrasts of the copytext. The text of Q1 is in black letter and its stage directions in roman type; italic and roman type are used for contrast. In this edition the text is in roman type with italics for proper names and other words specially designated by the typography of Q1; the reverse is true of stage directions. As in Q1,

character designations other than proper names are not set in contrasting
type in stage directions (e.g. "Shrive"). As the speeches locate the
scenes adequately for the dramatist's purpose, no editorial locations are
recorded. Q1 has no scene numbers; they are added in this edition at
each change of locale. Because the division into two parts is arbitrary,
the scenes are numbered consecutively throughout.

References to the text consist of scene and line numbers (e.g. iv.
10); stage directions within a scene are keyed decimally to the preceding
line; stage directions beginning a scene are keyed decimally as in this
example: i.0.2.

Most glosses in the explanatory notes are based on the definitions
and quotations of the OED, unless otherwise noted.

II   THE DATE

The title page of Q1 fixes 1591 as a posterior limit for the date of
the Raigne; no one has questioned its reliability. January 1587 (New
Style), the date of the second edition of Holinshed, is an anterior limit:
the play's direct debt to Holinshed is certain, and the first edition has
no account of King John.

None of the other evidence which I have seen[24] narrows these limits

[24]Frederick Gard Fleay, Shakespeare Manual (London: Macmillan, 1876), p. 88,
Chronicle History of the Life and Works of William Shakespeare (London: John
C. Nimmo, 1886), p. 27, A Biographical Chronicle of the English Drama 1559-
1642, 2 vols. (London: Reeves and Turner, 1891), II, 52; Hermann Ulrici,
Shakespeare's Dramatic Art, trans. from the 3rd German edition by L. Dora
Schmitz, 2 vols. (London: George Bell, 1889), II, 379; William Dinsmore
Briggs, "Introduction," Marlowe's Edward II (London: David Nutt, 1914), p.
lxxxvi; E. K. Chambers, "The Date of Marlowe's Tamburlaine," TLS, August 28,
1930, p. 684; Rupert Taylor, "A Tentative Chronology of Marlowe's and Some
Other Elizabethan Plays," PMLA, LI (1936), 648; T. W. Baldwin, Shakspere's
Five-Act Structure (Urbana: University of Illinois Press, 1947), p. 772;
Hereward T. Price, review of Marlowe and the Early Shakespeare by F. P. Wil-
son, Shakespeare Quarterly, V (1954), 183; Matthew P. McDiarmid, "Concerning

certainly; the Raigne may have been written any time between January
1586/7 and March 1591/2. But other considerations affect the date,
especially the sources and authorship. If Shakespeare's King John
turned out to be a source of the Raigne we could not date the anonymous
play much before 1591 without revising much of current thinking about
Shakespeare's early chronology. Or if the claim for Shakespeare as
author were seriously entertained it would be tempting to push its date
back as far as possible towards the anterior limit. But if we avoid
relying on these considerations in discussing date, what can be concluded otherwise about date may be brought to the puzzles of source and
authorship without circular reasoning.

III   THE SOURCES

Several contemporary accounts of King John resemble one another so
closely that it is difficult to tell whether their connection with the
Raigne is direct, indirect, or collateral. Significant parallels without analogue in other sources have established several direct debts, but
so much of the material of the Raigne is shared in the sources that no
single influence is clearly dominant. This is especially true as long
as the priority of Shakespeare's King John cannot be rejected
conclusively.

'The Troublesome Reign of King John,'" Notes and Queries, CCII (1957),
435; T. W. Baldwin, On the Literary Genetics of Shakspere's Plays: 1592-
1594 (Urbana: University of Illinois Press, 1959), p. 210; J. C. Maxwell,
"Introduction," Titus Andronicus (New Arden ed.) 3rd ed. (London: Methuen;
Cambridge, Mass.: Harvard University Press, 1961), pp. xxii-xxiii; Andrew
S. Cairncross, "Introduction," The Third Part of King Henry VI, New Arden
ed. (London: Methuen; Cambridge, Mass.: Harvard University Press, 1964),
pp. xliv-xlv; Irving Ribner, The English History Play in the Age of
Shakespeare, rev. ed. (New York: Barnes and Noble, 1965), p. 77.

1. Shakespeare's King John

Peter Alexander's suggestion that Shakespeare's King John might be[25] a source of The Troublesome Raigne evidently originated with two circumstances: the discovery of "good" and "bad" quartos, and the technical unevenness of the Raigne. For a time the play passed without question as a good quarto because it lacks most of the earmarks of the bad. But W. J. Courthope had claimed that its structure, among other things, marked it as an early work of Shakespeare's—an opinion which Wilson calls "one of the curiosities of criticism" (p. xix), presumably because, as E. M. W. Tillyard observes, "the masterly construction is quite at odds with the heterogeneous execution."[26] This unevenness prompted Alexander to suggest that the Raigne was not the source of Shakespeare, but a derivation:

Powers of construction and integration . . . cannot be acquired, though they may be developed. Yet it is precisely here that the author of The Troublesome Raigne is supposed to have shown the way to Shakespeare. In all that can be put under the heading of vocabulary or versification or atmosphere the plays are worlds apart; in their construction and unity of impression they are as close together as two very differing pieces can be.[27]

Most critics remain convinced that the Raigne was written first, but the evidence is not really conclusive either way. In 1953 F. P. Wilson

---

[25] Alexander is less dogmatic than some of his disciples; to his argument from the structure of the Raigne he adds a reservation: "The whole question . . . must be considered still an open one. . . . The simpler explanation need not necessarily be the true one, and The Troublesome Raigne may be just another of those things that criticism, even in its dreams, finds it difficult to imagine" (Alexander's Introductions to Shakespeare, London and Glasgow: Collins, 1964, p. 99).

[26] Shakespeare's History Plays (Harmondsworth: Penguin, 1962), p. 216.

[27] Alexander's Introductions, p. 99. Cf. his Shakespeare's Life and Art (London: James Nisbet, 1939), p. 85. But Tillyard's alternative (p. 216 ff.) is more plausible.

reserved judgment:

I see nothing unlikely or offensive in the orthodox view that The Troublesome Reign is a play which Shakespeare rewrote when he had found his
'new style' about the time in the mid-fifteen-nineties that he wrote
Richard II. . . . Yet we still await the proof that The Troublesome Reign
is earlier or later than King John . . . , and such evidence as I have
seen seems reversible or inconclusive.[28]

Most of the arguments on both sides are variations on one of a handful

of basic lines of reasoning; a summary of these will show what good war-

rant still remains for skepticism.

(a) Bad Quarto Earmarks

As Wilson observes, "From the bibliographical point of view The

Troublesome Reign is not a 'bad' quarto" (p. xx). Kenneth Muir finds it

"incredible that hack writers who were so well acquainted with Shake-

speare's play as to follow it scene by scene could reproduce none of the

actual dialogue."[29] So Honigmann suggests a different derivation, such

as that which Alexander envisaged for A Shrew; and he quotes Alexander's

illustration--Tate Wilkinson's reconstruction of Sheridan's Duenna: "I

locked myself in my room; set down first all the jokes I remembered, then

I laid a book of the songs before me; and with magazines kept the reg-

ulation of the scenes; and by the help of a numerous collection of ob-

solete Spanish plays, I produced an excellent comic Opera" (Honigmann,

p. liv). This sorts well with what we find when we compare the two plays

and consider the probable conditions of composition. The belief that

the author of the Raigne could not likely have had access to a text of

King John (Wilson, p. xxxii) fits Honigmann's picture of an extra-

ordinary piracy; so do some of Wilson's reasons for rejecting the Raigne

as a typical bad quarto. He thinks it

[28]Marlowe and the Early Shakespeare (Oxford: Clarendon Press, 1953), p. 115.

[29]"Source Problems in the Histories," Shakespeare-Jahrbuch, XCVI (1960), 50.

difficult to understand why the author . . . should have completely
stripped the play of all its poetry and taken the trouble to dress it
up in fustian verse of his own; should have reconstructed the whole in
the light of an independent reading of the chronicles, so that he produced a text which followed them far more closely than Shakespeare himself had done; and should have gone out of his way not only to infuse
the play with a strong anti-Catholic bias but also to substitute a
harassed, if erring, martyr-king for Shakespeare's sinister John; and
all this in order to prepare copy for a publisher, who could not have
given him more than a few shillings for his pains! [p. xxxii]

An author with only a scenario abstracted from performance must have

been an extraordinary person to reproduce more of the original language

than the sort of brief and haphazard parallels which Wilson cites (pp.

xxvi-xxxi), and no typical hack could reproduce Shakespeare's charac-

ters. Reading the chronicles would be a very useful substitute for

Shakespeare's situations and dialogue. The political and religious

intent of the play is clear both in martyr-king and in anti-Catholic

bias; and profit might not concern a public crusader.

Because Honigmann makes The Troublesome Raigne a reconstruction

based neither on stenography nor on actors' memories, he does not need

to regard it as a bad quarto. But his term "derivative play" (p. lvi)

enforces the distinction less clearly than Gary's label "plot-based

adaptation" (p. 20 ff.); and insisting on "some recognized 'bad quarto'

characteristics" (p. lvii) invites his reader to consider the play as

a typical bad quarto, while his reasons are not convincing (pp. lv-

lviii, 174-175). The argument is irrelevant.

(b) Circumstances of Origin

Critics on both sides of the priority question have appealed to external

evidence. Arguing for the precedence of King John, Alexander says:

For King John there is no entry of any kind in the Stationers' Register
before its inclusion in the First Folio. Heminge and Condell treated
the publication of The Troublesome Raigne as authorizing the printing of
King John, a claim which could hardly have been maintained had The Troub-

lesome Raigne been an original play by an author other than
Shakespeare.[30]

But the Raigne had been published as Shakespeare's in 1622 (before the
completion of the First Folio); the stationers may well have thought
that Shakespeare wrote both versions.

M. M. Reese appeals to external evidence on the other side: "[It
was not] the usual practice of actors who plundered someone else's play
for their own use, usually in the provinces, to lengthen the text and
enlarge the cast."[31] But the Raigne may not have been pirated for the
provinces; and its speaking parts could be discharged by an ordinary
company. And Honigmann conjectures that "the printer's copy may have
been padded with interpolations to disguise the shortness of the two
parts" (p. 176); Melun's dying speech and parts of the meeting at St.
Edmund's shrine might be suspected. Or a pirate might introduce these
passages, and the three-hundred-odd lines given to the monastics, to
emphasize his political and religious themes. Gary offers an impressive
rationale for additions to Shakespeare (pp. 49-60), illustrating from
A Shrew, the Contention, and the first quarto of Hamlet how pirated
copies tended to dramatize actions which Shakespeare only reports: a
situation which resembles most of the Raigne's additions.

Robert Adger Law suggests other evidence for the priority of the
Raigne: "It is significant that no such fraud [as the ascription to
Shakespeare in Q2 and Q3] is attempted on the title-page of either Part
of the 1591 Quarto. Ten years later [sic] it first appeared."[32] But

[30] Shakespeare (London and New York: Oxford University Press, 1964), pp.
170-171.

[31] The Cease of Majesty (London: E. Arnold; New York: St. Martin's Press,
1961), p. 265, n. 1.

[32] "On the Date of King John," Studies in Philology, LIV (1957), 120.

Shakespeare's name meant more in 1611 than in 1591. Law also notes:
"Records show that Elizabethan plays were not usually published in the
year that they were first acted. Thus the further back we push the as-
sumed second play, the earlier must be the date of the first" (p. 120),
and the difficulties for Shakespeare's chronology are increased. But if
the Raigne (though fitted for the stage) were written primarily to be
published and passed off as the King John of Shakespeare, produced by
the Queen's men, the first performance of King John might antedate the
Raigne only by the time required for the writing and printing. Still,
chronology is perhaps the main problem for the revisionists: if King
John is a source for the Raigne its date must be moved back from the
mid-nineties to at least 1591. Law quickly disposes of Honigmann's
"topical allusions" in King John: almost all are also in the Raigne.[33]
Wilson, proposing that Shakespeare wrote King John in 1590 from a
prompt-copy of the Raigne and later revised it (pp. xxxiii, lii-lv),
offers other arguments for early dating. First, "successful perform-
ances of a King John play on the London stage at this time [1590] would
give point to the publication of The Troublesome Reign in 1591" (p.
liv). But the Raigne itself might be that play. Second, he cites contemporary allusions which "all point to the early nineties" (p. lii);
his inferences are plausible, not inevitable.

The critics of Honigmann's dating need positive evidence. Chambers' date, 1596-97 (I, 366), depends on the larger hypothesis of his
whole chronology, which may influence ideas about King John more than
the facts strictly warrant. The conclusion of Law's essay is an
illustration:

[33]"On the Date of King John," pp. 125-126.

Gradually, by piecing together bits of fact and careful distinction between the known and the unknown, we have come to recognize more and more
clearly the development of the author's poetic and dramaturgic art and so
to interpret what he wrote. To trace this growth properly we must depend
on the material he had and the order in which he constructed his works.
Without compelling reason we should not be ready to upturn the very founda-
tions on which the whole structure is built.[34]

This edifice, however, is not built wholly of fact; one still unknown

point is the date of King John. Beyond the mere love of certainty there

is no urgent necessity for a complete Shakespeare chronology; a picture

of Shakespeare's development is not worth having if it is built on guess-

work. In any case, Honigmann's theory does not need to alter the tradi-

tional order of Shakespeare's plays, if their dates can be revised to a

somewhat earlier schedule. The facts in Chambers' chronology by them-

selves provide no reliable anterior limit for King John beyond that im-

plied by Shakespeare's birth date.[35] Chambers calls 1591 (his tentative

date for 2 and 3 Henry VI) "the earliest year to which there is ground

for ascribing any dramatic work by Shakespeare that we know of" (I, 59).

But for our purposes this is argument from ignorance. The other objec-

tions I have found do not make the case impossible, though they suggest

what revision of view would follow if the priority of King John should

be firmly established.

A clear anterior limit for King John after 1591 would prove that

the Raigne was written first. Arthur Freeman tries to reverse Wilson's

[34]"On the Date of King John," p. 127.

[35]Hence Honigmann's appeal to his critics "to suspend preconceptions about
dates until all the other evidence, judged per se, can be weighed," because "the debated John-T.R. relationship must necessarily be a mainstay
of either chronological theory" (p. liii). This is true of either theory,
taken as a whole with the conjectures needed to stick its facts together.
Rather than ignoring dates I prefer to abstract the facts from the systems.

argument from a parallel with Soliman and Perseda: "If . . . Solyman can

be dated after 1591, then the early date for John is rendered impossible,

and Troublesome Raigne cannot be a bad quarto."[36] He finds reason to

date the play 1591-92. But if Soliman made a proverb of knighthood and

Basilisco (which Shakespeare's Bastard repeats), it might well have been

added to King John for a revival. Charles Petit-Dutaillis tries to fix

1598 as the anterior limit for King John, quoting the Bastard's reaction

to the "commodity" of John's "most base and vile-concluded peace" (II.i.

586) before Angiers:

Apparently Shakespeare was influenced by the breach between Elizabeth and
Henry IV [of France]. The king of France was in the act of coming to
terms with the king of Spain, Elizabeth's sworn enemy, in the peace signed
at Vervins in 1598; and this, incidentally, induced me to suggest 1598 as
the date of the composition and production of King John.[37]

But such a parallel and others like it[38] may be accidental.

A more serious difficulty is implied in Marco Mincoff's revision of

Chambers' dates for the early plays;[39] since Mincoff argues that "Shake-

speare's rate of production was about two plays to a season" (p. 253)

even his revised dating does little to accommodate King John by 1591.

And F. P. Wilson raises the formidable objection of style: "We shall have

to reconcile, if we can, the maturity of so much in King John with the

---

[36]"Shakespeare and 'Solyman and Perseda,'" Modern Language Review, LVIII
(1963), 483.

[37]"Un héros shakespearien; le Bâtard de Falconbridge," Académe des inscrip-
tions & belles-lettres: comptes rendus des séances de l'année 1943 (Paris:
Henri Didier, 1943), p. 524 (my translation).

[38]See G. B. Harrison, "Shakespeare's Topical Significances," TLS, November
13, 1930, p. 939.

[39]"The Chronology of Shakespeare's Early Works," Shakespeare-Jahrbuch, C-CI
(1964-65), 253-265. He suggests: 1 H.VI, 1589; Shrew, 2 H.VI, 1590; 3 H.VI,
Errors, 1591; Tit., T.G.V., 1592; Venus, L.L.L., 1593; Lucr., R.III, 1594.

immaturity of _Venus_ _and_ _Adonis_ and _Lucrece_ of 1592-4. No arguments about

the difference between dramatic and non-dramatic verse could make that

palatable."[40] But a remark of Coleridge's may solve both problems:

> We are tolerably certain, indeed, that the Venus and Adonis, and the Rape
> of Lucrece, were his two earliest poems, and though not printed until
> 1593, . . . yet there can be little doubt that they had remained by him
> in manuscript many years. . . . Who can believe that Shakspeare could
> have remained to his twenty-ninth or thirtieth year without attempting
> poetic composition of any kind?[41]

If _King_ _John_ were written in 1591 considerations of style would require

still earlier dates for most of the works in Mincoff's list. If the play

as we have it were written in 1591 Shakespeare was hard at work in the

late eighties. The chief difficulty with such early dates for the first

plays is to harmonize them with the known limits for other plays, especi-

ally Marlowe's; Honigmann's introduction to _King_ _John_ fails to face up

squarely to this problem. But so little is known for certain that 1591

is not yet impossible. Wilson's view of _King_ _John_ provides another way

out: Shakespeare wrote _King_ _John_ in 1590 and revised it in 1594 (pp. lv-

lvi); this is a possibility as long as Chambers' date is unproved. Sub-

stantial evidence of a late anterior limit may have been overlooked

hitherto because the _Raigne_ was the unquestioned limit; but the same may

be said for evidence to the contrary. On external evidence the priority

of the _Raigne_ is yet an open question.

(c) _Internal_ _Evidence_

Is it possible to determine from the play itself that the _Raigne_

must, or must not, have come first? Wilson claims that _King_ _John_ must

be the later, because "direct access to the chronicles is an illusion"

---

[40] _Marlowe_ _and_ _the_ _Early_ Shakespeare, p. 117.

[41] _Shakespeare_ Criticism, ed. Thomas Middleton Raysor, 2 vols. (London:
Dent; New York: Dutton, 1960), I,. 209.

(p. xxxii). But Honigmann convincingly refutes this view; in addition

to the examples in his introduction (pp. xii-xviii) his notes cite two

parallels between King John and Holinshed which have no counterpart in

the Raigne:

> Old men and beldams in the streets
> Do prophesy upon it dangerously:
> Young Arthur's death is common in their mouths. . . .

John, IV.ii.185-187

For the space of fifteen daies this rumor [of Arthur's death] incessantlie
ran through both the realmes of England and France. . . .

Holinshed, III, 165, ii

> Be of good comfort, prince; for you are born
> To set a form upon that indigest
> Which he hath left so shapeless and so rude.

John, V.vii.25-27

A maruell it was to consider here at home, in how short a space the state
of the English common-wealth was changed, and from a troubled fourme reduced to a flourishing and prosperous degree: chieflie by the diligent
heed and carefull prouision of the king himselfe.

Holinshed, III, 203, ii

Conceding that the Raigne also reveals direct debts to Holinshed (examples

follow below), Honigmann concludes that "comparison with the chronicles

provides us with no final answer" to the question of precedence (p. xix).

Yet he maintains that source-comparisons make Shakespeare's priority the

likely alternative:

We can still ask how accurately the sources were followed when both plays
handle the same material. Does one take over the words of the source and
the other paraphrase them? Does one transplant an episode from its correct context, the other leave it there? Or do both contain the words of
the source, one not using them in the sense of the source? While the
second writer could conceivably revert to the source again and again,
one is inclined to award the precedence to the accurate man. And, though
the T.R. includes facts not given in John, Shakespeare is the accurate
man in all the types of divergence that we have outlined. [Footnotes cite
examples of each kind.] Upholders of the traditional theory about the
relations of the two plays will have to ponder this [pp. xviii-xix].

Sometimes, of course, the less imaginative man is the one who follows

his source closely; with this reservation let us test Honigmann's prin-

ciple. We find that Shakespeare is not consistently "the accurate man."

Sometimes the Raigne quotes directly where Shakespeare paraphrases:

(i)
Surelie queene Elianor the kings mother was sore against hir nephue Arthur, . . . for that she saw if he were king, how his mother Constance
would looke to beare most rule within the realme of England. . . .

                         Holinshed, III, 158, i

    Elinor
        Her pride we know, and know her for a Dame
        That will not sticke to bring him to his ende,
        So she may bring her selfe to rule a Realme.

                         Raigne, i.54-56

    Elea. Out, insolent! thy bastard shall be king,
        That thou mayst be a queen, and check the world!

                         John, II.i.122-123

(ii)
[The kings of England and France] concluded an agreement, with a marriage to be had betwixt Lewes the sonne of king Philip, and the ladie
Blanch, daugher to Alfonso king of Castile the 8 of that name, & neece
to K. John by his sister Elianor.

                         Holinshed, III, 161, i

    Citizen
        The beauteous daughter of the King of Spaine,
        Neece to K. John, the lovely Ladie Blanche,
        Begotten on his Sister Elianor.

                         Raigne, ii.332-334

    Hub. That daughter there of Spain, the Lady Blanche,
        Is near to England. . . .

                         John, II.i.423-424

(iii)
But king Philip . . . determined not so to breake off his enterprise,
least it might be imputed to him for a great reproach to have beene at
such charges and great expenses in vaine.

                         Holinshed, III, 178, ii

<u>Lewes</u>
    Why <u>Pandulph</u>, hath K. <u>Philip</u> sent his sonne
    And been at such excessive charge in warres,
    To be dismist with words?

<u>Raigne</u>, xii.35-37

<u>Lew</u>. Am I Rome's slave? What penny hath Rome borne,
    What men provided, what munition sent,
    To underprop this action? Is't not I
    That undergo this charge?

<u>John</u>, V.ii.97-100

Likewise, alongside Honigmann's examples of his second point (epi-
sodes transplanted in the <u>Raigne</u>) we may set similar instances from
Shakespeare. First, Honigmann notes (on III.ii.6-7) that the rescue of
Elinor is placed among the feats of the Bastard, though Holinshed attributes it to swift and vigorous action on the part of John (III, 164).
But the <u>Raigne</u> follows Holinshed: "<u>Excursions</u>. Elianor <u>is</u> <u>rescued</u> <u>by</u>
John . . ." (iii.190.i). Second, in the dialogue following the capture
of Arthur the <u>Raigne</u> gives John a speech closely resembling the reports
of Matthew Paris and Holinshed on the same event; Shakespeare's John
says much the same thing, not after he has imprisoned Arthur, but during
the first encounter before Angiers:

Coepit eum rex blandis alloqui verbis et multos honores promittere, ex-
hortans ut a rege Francorum recederet, et sibi ut domino et avunculo
fideliter adhaereret. ["The king began to coax him with smooth words,
and to give him hope of many honors, urging him to forsake the King of
the French, and to stick faithfully to his lord and uncle" (my translation).]

Matthew Paris, II, 479

King John . . . went about to persuade him all that he could to forsake
his freendship and aliance with the French king, and to leane and sticke
to him being his naturall uncle.

Holinshed, III, 165, i

<u>K</u>. <u>John</u>
    But if at last, Nephew thou yeeld thy selfe
    Into the gardance of thine Unckle <u>John</u>,
    Thou shalt be used as becomes a Prince.

<u>Raigne</u>, iv.4-6

K. <u>John</u>. Arthur of Britain, yield thee to my hand;
    And out of my dear love I'll give thee more
    Than e'er the coward hand of France can win:
    Submit thee, boy.

                    <u>John</u>, II.i.156-159

Third, where Holinshed says that "Lewes, after he understood of this

mischance [the loss of the reinforcing fleet] . . . inclined the sooner

unto peace, so that at length he tooke such offers of agreement as were

put unto him" (III, 201, ii), Shakespeare makes him begin to withdraw

without a parley with the English, and offer his own terms of peace:

<u>Sal</u>. The Cardinal Pandulph is within at rest,
    Who half an hour since came from the Dolphin,
    And brings from him such offers of our peace
    As we with honour and respect may take,
    With purpose presently to leave this war.
<u>Bast</u>. He will the rather do it when he sees
    Ourselves well sinew'd to our defence.
<u>Sal</u>. Nay, 'tis in a manner done already,
    For many carriages he hath dispatch'd
    To the sea-side, and put his cause and quarrel
    To the disposing of the cardinal. . . .

                    <u>John</u>, V.vii.82-92

Though Lewis' reason in the <u>Raigne</u> differs from Holinshed, the basic

situation is the same as in the source:

<u>Henry</u>
    Answere in fine if thou wilt take a peace,
    And make surrender of my right againe,
    Or trie thy title with the dint of sword?
.   .   .   .

<u>Lewes</u>
    <u>Henry</u> of <u>England</u>, now that <u>John</u> is dead,
    That was the chiefest enemie to <u>Fraunce</u>,
    I may the rather be inducde to peace.

                    <u>Raigne</u>, xvi.10-12, 16-18

To illustrate his third question Honigmann cites two parallels.

"In both plays," he notes first (p. xii), "King Philip, like Holinshed,

comments on John's military speed: but only Shakespeare used 'looked for'

in the source's sense." Here are the relevant passages:

K. John commeth upon his enimies not looked for.

> Holinshed, III, 164, ii, margin

How much unlook'd for is this expedition!

> John, II.i.79

I rather lookt for some submisse reply. . . .

> Raigne, ii.78

The passage from Holinshed is a marginal summary of John's dispatch in rescuing his mother at Mirabeau--the account represented in both plays as John's last battle in France, ending with the capture of Arthur. But both lines from the plays belong to the first parley before Angiers, which is not in the chronicles. Precedence is indeterminate; each playwright could have borrowed the phrase independently, if it is borrowed. Honigmann's other example involves several points; on the calamity of the washes (Paris, II, 667) he says (p. xvi):

(i) Shakespeare's "Devoured by the . . . flood" (V.vii.64) = Matthew's "a fluctibus deuoratis"; the T.R. reads "The . . . tyde . . . swallowed", bringing in "flouds" further down; (ii) Shakespeare and Matthew make the disaster itself "unexpected"; in the T.R. the news of the disaster is "vnexpected"; (iii) Shakespeare's "hardly have escap'd" = Matthew's "vix elapsus"; the T.R. reads simply "escapt", like Holinshed; (iv) Shakespeare explains twice that the floods came at night, and Matthew seems to imply that; the T.R. gives the time as "morning"; (v) Holinshed and Foxe report this incident more briefly than Matthew, without any of the verbal parallels which we have italicized.

"Bringing in 'flouds' further down" is not an apt example of "not using [words] in the sense of the source"; and it is the eventu that is unexpected in the source, but the "flood" in King John (V.vii.64). Though the Raigne has no equivalent for vix, McDiarmid finds three other phrases from this passage which the Raigne translates and Shakespeare does not. [42] He also disagrees (pp. 436-437) with Honigmann on the time: "The anony-

[42] "Concerning 'The Troublesome Reign . . . ,'" 436.

mous writer . . . makes the loss occur in the morning, which is the
natural implication in Matthew's statement that John spent that night at
the abbey." But this is a matter of fact, not of verbal accuracy, and
it brings us to other questions like the three which Honigmann asks.

First, do both plays reproduce an episode, but the one with greater
detail and accuracy? Honigmann notes four such instances where Shakespeare is not "the accurate man": the Raigne and Holinshed represent
Peter the prophet as foretelling the deposition not to the public at
large (as in Shakespeare) but to the King; the Raigne and Holinshed make
Melun not a count (as in Shakespeare) but a viscount; the Raigne and
Holinshed provide the Earl of Pembroke's name, but Shakespeare does not;
and Arthur's age corresponds in the Raigne and Holinshed, but not in
King John (p. xviii, n. 4). Related to this last point is Arthur's attitude to the quarrel over his claim, on which Holinshed, Matthew Paris,
and the Raigne agree against Shakespeare:

Arthur like one that wanted good counsell, and abounding too much in his
own wilfull opinion, made a presumptuous answer [to John's appeal for submission and promise of honor], not onlie denieng so to doo, but also com-
manding king John to restore unto him the realme of England, with all
those other lands and possessions which king Richard had in his hand at
the houre of his death.
                              Holinshed, III, 165, i (translating
                                 the following passage)

Arthurus vero, stulto usus consilio, regi cum indignatione et comminatione
respondens, exegit ut redderet sibi regnum Angliae cum terris omnibus et
rebus, quas rex Ricardus habuit in possessione sua die qua decessit.

                              Matthew Paris, II, 479

·Arthur
     Might hath prevayld not right, for I am King
     Of England, though thou weare the Diadem.

                              Raigne, iv.9-10

Arth. I would that I were low laid in my grave:
     I am not worth this coil that's made for me.

                              John, II.i.164-165

Also, Melun's distress for the state of England is found both in Foxe

and in the Raigne:

I pittie poor England, which hath bene so noble a region, that now it is
come to so extreme misery.

Foxe, I, 225, ii

Melun
    Back warmen, back, imbowell not the clyme,
    Your seate, your nurse, your birth dayes breathing place,
    That bred you, beares you, brought you up in armes.
    Ah be not so ingrate to digge your Mothers grave,
    Preserve your lambes and beate away the Wolfe.

Raigne, xii.127-131

But though Shakespeare used the passage (cf. Honigmann on V.iv.42-43),

he comes no closer to Foxe's version than this:

Mel. Commend me to one Hubert with your king:
    The love of him, and this respect besides,
    For that my grandsire was an Englishman,
    Awakes my conscience to confess all this.

John, V.iv.40-43

Again, does one play transplant words from their correct context,

the other leave them there? In one case at least the Raigne comes off

better than King John:

The French king . . . with all diligence made his provision of men,
ships, munition, and vittell, in purpose to passe over into England.

Holinshed, III, 176, ii

Messenger
    For all thy forces being fiftie sayle,
    Conteyning twenty thousand souldyers,
    With victuall and munition for the warre,
    Putting from Callis in unluckie time,
    Did crosse the seas, and on the Goodwin sands,
    The men, munition, and the ships are lost.

Raigne, xiv.30-35

Lew. Am I Rome's slave? What penny hath Rome borne,
    What men provided, what munition sent,
    To underprop this action?

John, V.ii.97-99

Honigmann offers the alternatives of awarding "the precedence to the
accurate man," or picturing the second writer as achieving the greater
accuracy by "revert[ing] to the source again and again" instead of simply
following the earlier play. But it is not easy to choose the accurate
man. If John was written first the author of the Raigne frequently ignored Shakespeare's version for the chronicles. Such is not unlikekly
if he had no copy of Shakespeare; he could follow the historical sources
more closely than his predecessor, whose vagaries might be forgotten or
rejected. And Shakespeare might have found himself in a similar situation if he were indebted to the Raigne; Wilson observes that "had he
acted in it such an experience would entirely account for those innumer-
able little verbal echoes in King John which . . . are for the most part
obviously the result of unconscious tricks of memory" (p. xxxiii-xxxiv).
Thus we may accept, without Honigmann's reservations, his conclusion
that "comparison with the chronicles provides us with no final answer."

Wilson (pp. xxi-xxxiv) infers the priority of the Raigne from parallels which Shakespeare could have adapted from the Raigne, but which the
anonymous author could not have derived from King John. Honigmann
takes up seven such one-way parallels,[43] and demonstrates that they need
not be one-way (p. 171):

The "inconsistencies" in John can all be rejected, we think, on one or
more of four counts: (i) Shakespeare's vocabulary was not fully appreci-
ated; (ii) some of the "inconsistencies" are actually subtleties, and
the editors and not Shakespeare must be blamed for working too hurriedly;
(iii) the sources have been followed--without "misunderstandings"--so
that Shakespeare himself did not originate inconsistencies; (iv) various
"inconsistencies", laboriously searched for to prove the priority of the

---

[43]These are the Bastard's annoyance at the marriage of Blanch, the motivation for the poisoning of John, the reason for a meeting at St. Edmunds-
bury, John's reasons for the second coronation, his instructions to Hubert
about Arthur, the references of Constance to John as "perjur'd" and two
obscure expressions: "and the territories" (I.i.10) and "bank'd" (V.ii.104).

T.R., have numerous parallels in Shakespeare's other plays, and would
never have been so named if his customary techniques had been compared.

Honigmann dismisses other arguments by saying that "Wilson summarized

the key arguments of his predecessors" (p. 167), but they are objections

to be met individually.

For example, "Shakespeare was following The Troublesome Raigne

without any comprehension of the history upon which it was based"--so

concludes V. K. Whitaker,[44] from such apparent blunders as this: "Arth.

God shall forgive you Coeur-de-lion's death / The rather that you give

his offspring life" (II.i.12-13). But Honigmann shows Shakespeare's

reliance on Holinshed; and his note to this passage give Moberly's

explanation:

Shakespeare follow the language of official documents "in which kings
are held to be descended from their predecessors. So even Henry VII.
repeatedly speaks of 'our royal progenitor, King Edward the Fourth.'"

Matthew P. McDiarmid sees a one-way parallel in John's submitting

to Pandulph while believing Arthur to be alive, and his sending the

Bastard to reconcile the revolted barons "before Hubert makes his con-

fession and provides John with the only argument that could make Fal-

conbridge's embassy successful."[45] He infers that Shakespeare inherited

"a scheme that he could not adapt to his different conception without

evident distortion" (p. 438). As Honigmann says, some apparent "incon-

sistencies" are Shakespeare's subtleties. Here are signs in John of

panic and illogic like that of Richard III after Buckingham flees; the

Bastard recognizes it and tries to rouse him: "Be great in act, as you

have been in thought" (V.i.45).

[44]Shakespeare's Use of Learning (San Marino: Huntington Library, 1953),
p. 133.

[45]"Concerning 'The Troublesome Reign . . . ,'" 437.

J. Isaacs adduces other one-way parallels; one example will illustrate their tentative force as proof. The "three corners of the world"
(V.vii.116) must be derived from the last lines of the Raigne:[46] "If
Englands Peeres and people joyne in one, / Nor Pope, nor Fraunce, nor
Spaine can doo them wrong." But this commonplace could be found anywhere, once France (with a Catholic king once more) created imminent
danger of a three-way alliance against England. Isaacs calls Shakespeare's revision a "coalescing process" which "can only work in one
direction" (p. 127). But though he sees Shakespeare's improving hand
where King John excels the Raigne, he regards passages handled worse as
by-products of Shakespeare's "compression and revision" (p. 123). We
cannot have it both ways. Nor is there much to choose between the two.
Gary notes the tendency to polarize issues (pp. 74-79) and to fuse borrowings (pp. 83-101) in the Raigne as indications that it is derived
from Shakespeare; but her examples might well be Shakespeare's sophisti-
cation of issues, and expansion of borrowings, from the Raigne.

Noting that the anonymous author "has provided the rebels with the
combined motivations of all of John's various enemies,"[47] J. L. Simmons
argues for the priority of the Raigne (p. 66):

Shakespeare deliberately cuts away all except the nobles' genuine indig-
nation over Arthur's death as motivation for their rebellion, a simplicity he could not have derived directly from Holinshed. In the chronicle
Arthur's death was not an English concern at all, and only TR's conflation could make it so. Therefore, in what is the structural crux for
both plays, TR is recognizably close to Holinshed, but King John's relationship to the chronicle is hardly comprehensible without the intervening
accentuation of Arthur's death in conjunction with more purely historical
and political motivations.

It seems dangerous to assume that the conflation could not be Shakespeare's.

[46]"Shakespeare's Earliest Years in the Theatre," Proceedings of the Brit-
ish Academy, XXXIX (1953), 124.

[47]"Shakespeare's King John and Its Source: Coherence, Pattern, and Vision,"
Tulane Studies in English, XVII (1969), 65.

Honigmann makes a better case for one-way borrowings in the other direction (pp. 171-173). Not all of his examples admit no alternate explanation: the "contradiction" in the Raigne between Old Falconbridge's recognition of Philip as his heir and the six-week discrepancy in his account of the pregnancy may mean only that he was content to accept as a benefit from Providence any son born in wedlock; the Bastard's ignorance of his father is not really a contradiction, for his mother has never confirmed his suspicions;[48] and when Philip of France repeats his promises to Constance and betrays her almost in one breath, the author characterizes Philip and the French as treacherous (ii.366-370). But the citizens' request for a parley where they say nothing (ii.258-260, 265) is harder to explain. And Peter's prediction concerning the noon of Ascension Day (not in Holinshed or Foxe) makes a spectacular confusion:

An elaborate prophecy is "planted", its point is forgotten, the prepared "facts" are confused, and then, best of all, Shakespeare's threat to hang Peter on Ascension day at noon (IV. ii. 155-7), a threat not made in the T.R., is put into execution (T.R., II. ii. 43-5 [x.43-45], though the T.R. at this stage envisages another twelve hours before the end of the danger!

Much of the effect of this instance, however, disappears when one considers that Peter is put to death not because it is noon, but because John believes the danger is past and the prophet false: "Now John, thy feares are vanisht into smoake, / Arthur is dead, thou guiltlesse of his death" (x.47-48). Gary also infers (p. 60) that the Raigne is following King John because the Prophet is introduced to Part II without good reason. But he is not essential to the action anywhere: in both parts he simply evokes from John expressions of his expedient, and thus rapidly vacillating, attitude to Arthur's life. This case illustrates my feeling

---

[48]On reasoning similar to Honigmann's, Frank O'Connor suggested that the discovery of the Bastard in the trial was an interpolation made for a revival of the play (Shakespeare's Progress, New York: Collier, 1961, pp. 76-77). But the assumption that Philip's conference with his mother creates a redundancy is not a necessary one.

that five more cases (pp. 61-69) where Gary interprets the Raigne as
assuming knowledge of King John involve misunderstandings of the anonymous
play. Either view could be right--the whole line of reasoning is
inconclusive.

There is tantalizing evidence to be inferred from Shakespeare's
usual treatment of his sources. Arguing for the precedence of the
Raigne, Law notes that in the other histories he concentrates on "a few
years and a few pages of Holinshed," but in King John "the principle of
selectivity . . . is not used."[49] But Richard III covers fourteen years;
and the principle of selection in King John has long since[50] been noted:
everything turns on Arthur's fate. On the other view, if Shakespeare
used the Raigne he has included more than usual of his source's structure,
as Gary notes (p. 4), and less than usual of its language. Though King
John is different from the Raigne in pacing and proportion, especially
in Acts IV and V, the plots coincide, as Law admits (p. 125), "almost
precisely, scene by scene." Before we are too impressed it is worth noting that the question of priority began with the surprise of critics at
the solid structure of an otherwise undistinguished play. If there is
anything unusual in this relation of King John to its presumed source,
it may just be that for once Shakespeare found a satisfactory plot. It
is harder to explain away the paucity of verbal parallels; Gary demonstrates that from Shakespeare we might expect more affinities even in
speech heads (pp. 41-42). The theory of plot-based derivation fits this
internal evidence better than the traditional view.

[49]Law, "On the Date of King John, " 125.

[50]"Supplementary Notice" [to John], The Pictorial Edition of the Works
of Shakspere, ed. Charles Knight, 8 vols. (London, 1839-42), IV, 358-359.

A final answer to the question of precedence is more likely through internal evidence than by other known means, if enough study and consideration can be brought to it. At present confident conclusions would be premature.[51]

2. Other Sources

The Raigne reveals other direct influences besides Holinshed and Matthew Paris; one could be the Actes and Monuments of John Foxe. According to Elson,

the circumstantial account given by Foxe has the following points found in T.R. but not in Holinshed:
1. the monk first takes counsel with his abbot concerning his contemplated murder.
2. The abbot praises the monk and absolves him in advance of the deed.
3. The monk obtains his poison from what he calls in the play "the inwards of a toad."
4. The monk speaks of his drink as one that "shall make all England glad" (in T.R. he calls it "the meriest draught y^t euer was dronk in England").
5. He uses the word "Wassail" in reference to the drink (as a name for it in Foxe, as the familiar drinker's cheer in T.R.).
6. The king pledges the monk in return for the latter's toast (only this element is mentioned in Holinshed).[52]

McDiarmid cites the following parallel:[53]

[51]Virginia Mason Carr concurs: "At this point, no one can say for certain what is the TR's relationship to KJ," "A Critical Reading of The Troublesome Reign of King John" (unpublished Ph.D. dissertation, University of Michigan, 1972), p. 152. But William H. Matchett is "convinced that [King John] preceded The Troublesome Reign," "A Note on the Text [of King John]," The Complete Signet Classic Shakespeare, ed. Sylvan Barnet (New York: Harcourt Brace Jovanovich, 1972), p. 564. Tillyard's postulate of an early Shakespeare play as the source of both extant plays (p. 216 ff.) would explain inconsistencies in both, and the unevenness of the Raigne. But even if all agreed on this as the "supposition best able to explain the facts" (p. 217), the theory would have little practical value without corroboration.

[52]"Studies in the King John Plays," in Joseph Quincy Adams Memorial Studies, ed. James G. McManaway et al. (Washington: The Folger Shakespeare Library, 1948), p. 189. Elson cites other parallels, some avowedly inconclusive.

[53]"Concerning 'The Troublesome Reign . . . ,'" p. 435.

Since I submitted my selfe and my lands, England and Ireland to the church
of Rome (sorrow come to it) never thing prospered with me, but all hath
gone against me.

                        Foxe, I, 225, ii

> John
>   Since John did yeeld unto the Priest of Rome,
>   Nor he nor his have prospred on the earth, . . .

                        Raigne, xv.95-96

And Dominic (pp. 38-40) cites the deceit of John's submission to Rome, the

motive of conscience in Melun's dying confession, and John's forgiveness

of the revolted barons on his deathbed--all in Foxe, but not in Holinshed.

But Richard Grafton's Chronicle at Large (1568, 1569) could have

provided this material in its extensive quotations from the first edi-

tion of Foxe (1563). I know of only one detail supposedly peculiar to

Foxe and the Raigne which Grafton does not also supply. A page of illus-

trations in Foxe shows the monk giving King John the cup of poison, and

saying "Wassail my lige"; but the apparent echo in the Raigne (xv.31) may

be merely coincidental since in Grafton's text the monk says: "I trust

this wassail shall make all England glad." And there is better evidence

that the author of the Raigne did consult Grafton, whose account of the

original French challenge and of Arthur's subsequent capture comes closer

to the action of the Raigne than anything in Holinshed, Paris, Stow, Foxe,

or Fabyan:

The French king required of king John that he shoulde depart with all his
landes in Normandy, and Pictavia, and else where within the dominion of
Fraunce, unto Arthure his nephew, and that incontinent, or else he woulde
warre against him, and foorthwith made great provision for warre, and
joyning with him the sayd Arthur, with a great army and puyssance, set
upon certeyne of his townes and Castels in Normandy, and put him to much
unquietnesse. When king John heard of this, he forthwith assembled a
counsail, and prayed an ayde against the French king, which was graunted
unto him. And with all spede possible prepared an army and sailed over,
and gave an onset on his enemies with such force (as by the provision of
almightie God the gever of all victory) the French king and his complices
had such a repulse at the English mennes handes, that they pursuying the

French men, in their flight did so nerely follow them into their holde,
and so enforced upon them, that they not onely tooke the said Arthur
prisoner, with manye other of the Frenche men, but also gave such an overthrow to the rest, that none was there left to beare tydynges home.[54]

Here are direct verbal parallels with the Raigne (e.g. "We meane with
speede to passe the sea to Fraunce," i.72), and there is more basis
here than elsewhere for the embassy of Chattilion. The French scenes of
the play may well be a conflation of this account with Holinshed's version of Arthur's claims (derived from Matthew Paris); but since other
explanations are possible, we cannot tell whether the author of the Raigne
consulted Foxe or Grafton or both.

The case of Polydore Vergil's Anglica Historica is less clear; Elson
suggests parallels, but none carries complete conviction (pp. 195-197).
The author of the Raigne and Vergil make more of the pathos of Lady Constance than Holinshed or Foxe, but they might do so independently. The
same is true of the comparisons of John to a madman. And the correspondences between the versions of the Bastard's escape from the washes could
be only coincidental: "Vergil . . . mentions the invasion of the sea,
whereas Holinshed uses only the vaguer phrase, 'the violence of the
waters.' And Vergil emphasizes especially the 'spirited and active horse'
. . . , whereas Holinshed says nothing of the guide's having a horse at
all" (pp. 196-197). On such evidence the debt to Vergil must be uncertain.

Apparently the author of the Raigne made no direct use of Stow or
Fabyan, but Edward Hall's story of Dunois, the Bastard of Orleans, is
sometimes thought to have supplied inspiration for the judicial discovery
of the Bastard. In similar litigation over an inheritance Dunois tells
the court: "My harte geveth me, & my noble corage telleth me, that I am

[54]A Chronicle at large and meere History of the affayres of Englande and
Kinges of the same (1569), II, 97-98.

the sonne of the noble Duke of Orleaunce, more glad to be his Bastarde,
with a meane livyng, then the lawfull sonne of that coward cuckolde
Cauny, with his foure thousande crounes."[55] Bullough thinks the incident a probable source for both King John and the Raigne, noting that
"Shakespeare would read it for 1H6" (p. 54, n. 2); but one wonders why
the author of the Raigne should bother to read Hall, whose history ex-
cludes the reign of John;[56] again the resemblance may be fortuitous, or
the influence indirect.

Such a verdict is almost certainly the one required for the claim
concerning Bale's Kynge Johan. Because the play is thought to have
existed only in manuscript in 1591,[57] "on general grounds" W. W. Greg
thinks it "very unlikely that the anonymous author should have been acquainted with Bale's manuscript."[58] Much of the apparent similarity is
due to Holinshed, Paris, and especially Foxe, whose verbal parallels
with Bale's poisoning scene are certainly more than accidental (though
they may be transmitted indirectly). Elson cites resemblances shared
only by Bale and the Raigne, but they can be explained without assuming
direct debt. First, the parallel comparisons of John with King David of
Israel (pp. 192-193) are not really parallel: Bale depicts John as the
boy David striking down "Great Golye the pope" with his sling; the Raigne
draws an analogy between John's inability to root out popery because of

---

[55] The Union of the Two Noble and Illustre Famelies of Lancastre and Yorke
(1548), cv.

[56] This fact might suggest the precedence of Shakespeare.

[57] The Malone Society's King Johan (Oxford University Press, 1931), p. vi,
records an enigmatic manuscript reference to an early edition, but apparently nothing further is known about it.

[58] "Bale's Kynge Johan," Modern Language Notes, XXXVI (1921), 505.

his sins and the divine prohibition against David's building the temple.[59]

Second, Elson refers to ten parallels in the poisoning scene; but if his illustration of them is representative, they are inconclusive:

> I hope in a whyle, to wurke some feat abroade.
>
> ### Kynge Johan, 1964
>
> For now my Lord I goe about my worke.
>
> ### Raigne, xiii.145

Third, he notes that "friendly speeches of John to the monk are found in Bale, as in T.R., whereas Foxe quotes only the monk" (p. 194); but if the author of the Raigne once decided to reproduce the monk's words from Foxe, some response in kind from John seems predictable in a dramatization. Finally Elson points out that both plays represent King John as desiring food or drink; again, this seems a predictable preparation for the poisoning. Elson says: "I am not prepared to maintain with certainty that Bale's Kyng Johan is indeed a source of T.R." (p. 191).

The certain direct sources of the Raigne are Paris, Holinshed, and one or both of Foxe and Grafton; Polydore Vergil, Hall, and Shakespeare's King John are unproven possibilities.

IV   THE AUTHORSHIP

Largely on internal evidence the Raigne has been attributed to Drayton, Greene, Kyd, Lodge, Marlowe, Munday, Peele, Rowley, and Shakespeare. But the verbal-parallel game is next to impossible if one observes Muriel

---

[59] Raigne, xv.98-107; I Chronicles xxii.7-8 (Geneva version, 1560): "And David said to Salomon, My sonne, I purposed with my selfe to buyld an house to the Name of the Lord my God, But the worde of the Lord came to me, saying, Thou hast shed muche blood, & hast made great battels: thou shalt not buylde an house unto my Name: for thou hast shed muche blood upon the earth in my sight."

St. C. Byrne's sensible rules.[60]Many aspects of vocabulary, of situation,

and of allusion, unusual verse meters, and special dramatic devices such

as the letter have been adduced as evidence fruitlessly,[61] because they

are all readily imitable: Courthope plausibly suggests that the author

of the Raigne imitates Marlowe's characterization, Peele's "ranting man-

ner," and Greene's "comic manner."[62] Some quantitative methods of attri-

bution[63] promise better days for internal evidence, but they are (often

avowedly) inconclusive as yet.

[60]"Bibliographical Clues in Collaborate Plays," The Library, 4th ser.,
XIII (1932-33), 21-48.

[61]Fleay, Biographical Chronicle of the English Drama, II, 52-53 (Peele,
Marlowe, Lodge, Greene); Hopkinson, pp. viii-xii (Marlowe, Lodge, Greene);
John MacKinnon Robertson, An Introduction to the Study of the Shakespeare
Canon (London: G. Routledge; New York: E. P. Dutton, 1924), pp. 278-287,
401-402 (Peele, Marlowe, Lodge, and Greene, or perhaps Drayton); William
Wells, "Thomas Kyd and the Chronicle-History," Notes and Queries, CLXXVIII
(1940), 218-224, 238-243 (Kyd); Paul V. Rubow, King John, Historisk-filo-
sofiske Medelelser udgivet af Det Kongelige Danske Videnskabernes Selskab,
Bind 37, nr. 9 (Copenhagen: I kommission hos Munksgaard, 1960), pp. 14-21
(Kyd); Georg Kopplow, Shakespeares „King John" und seine Quelle (Kiel,
1900), p. 40 ff. (Kyd); E. H. C. Oliphant, "How Not to Play the Game of
Parallels," Journal of English and Germanic Philology, XXVIII (1929), 7
(Peele and others); Ulrici, Shakespeare's Dramatic Art, II, 382 (cites
Von Friesen's suggestion of Peele and Greene); J. H. Ingram, Christopher
Marlowe and His Associates (London: Grant Richards, 1904), pp. 167-169
(Greene and Marlowe); W. L. Courtney, "Christopher Marlowe," Fortnightly
Review CCCCLXVI (October, 1905), 683 (Marlowe and Shakespeare); E. A.
Gerrard, Elizabethan Drama and Dramatists 1583-1603 (Oxford: University
Press, 1928), p. 189 (Munday); Munro, p. xiii (author of Leir); Wilson,
p. xvii (author of Edward I).

[62]A History of English Poetry (London: Macmillan, 1911), IV, 464-465.

[63]Alfred Hart, "Acting Versions of Elizabethan and Jacobean Plays," and
"The Vocabulary of Edward III," in Shakespeare and the Homilies and Other
Pieces of Research into the Elizabethan Drama (Melbourne: Melbourne Uni-
versity Press; London: Oxford University Press, 1934), pp. 119-153, 219-
241; Harold G. McCurdy, The Personality of Shakespeare (New Haven: Yale
University Press, 1953), pp. 47-76; J. C. Maxwell, "Peele and Shakespeare:
A Stylometric Test," Journal of English and Germanic Philology, XLIX
(1950), 557-560; Philip W. Timberlake, The Feminine Ending in English
Blank Verse (Menasha, Wisconsin: George Banta, 1931); Frederick O. Waller,
"The Use of Linguistic Criteria in Determining the Copy and Dates for
Shakespeare's Plays," in Pacific Coast Studies in Shakespeare (Eugene,
Oregon: University of Oregon, 1966), pp. 1-19; G. Udny Yule, The Statist-
ical Study of Literary Vocabulary (Cambridge: Cambridge University Press,
1944).

The best evidence is negative; solid objections to the claims for
Peele, Marlowe, and Shakespeare illustrate the difficulties in assigning
the Raigne to any known author. H. D. Sykes argued that it must be
Peele's because it is "a rambling production, very loosely constructed."[64]
As Arthur M. Sampley notes, however, "The value of plot structure as a
test for authorship is, I think, very strong negatively, but not quite
so strong when applied positively. So far as we know, Peele did not
write well-constructed plays; on the other hand, he cannot be held responsible for all the poorly constructed anonymous drama of his period."[65]
And any more favorable notion of the Raigne's structure works against
Sykes's view. "Though a good mask-writer," Wells observes,

Peele was a dramatist of little distinction, and it is difficult to see
how he could have written so, on the whole, well-constructed a play as
the 'Raigne' some two years before 'Edward I'--as Mr. Sykes claimed that
he did--that mere farrago of tomfoolery in which some historical person-
ages were compelled to take ignoble parts.[66]

William Wells and Irving Ribner invoke another negative criterion. Wells
points out that neither Greene nor Peele "paid serious attention to historical verities. On the contrary, history to them was but a peg on
which to hang some fanciful romance" (p. 218). Ribner sees in the
"romantic folk-lore" of Edward I "a tendency away from the serious treatment of history which we have noted in The Troublesome Raigne";[67] and he
holds that "as history plays, the works are so different both in intention

[64]Sidelights on Shakespeare (Stratford-upon-Avon: Shakespeare Head Press,
1919), p. 102.

[65]"Plot Structure in Peele's Plays as a Test of Authorship," PMLA, LI
(1936), 701.

[66]"Thomas Kyd and the Chronicle-History," Notes and Queries, CLXXVIII
(1940), 222.

[67]The English History Play, p. 89.

and accomplishment that it is difficult to conceive of their having been
written by the same person" (p. 77).

Beyond a few unfounded conjectures (the Raigne's allusion to Tamburlaine in the prefatory verses has been taken as proof that Marlowe
did,[68] and that he did not,[69] write the play), the evidence for Marlowe's
claim is mainly negative. On the two parts of the Raigne Marion Bodwell
Smith observes:

The imagery pattern of these plays is utterly unlike Marlowe's and the
images themselves are, in respect of style, at the opposite pole from
his. The great majority of the images in The Troublesome Reign are from
sources of which Marlowe seldom made use; nor do we find, in either part,
more than a few vague echoes of his actual figures.[70]

A. H. Bullen observed: "Earless and unabashed must be the critic who would
charge Marlow with any complicity in The Troublesome Reign of King John."[71]
Most significant is not the sprinkling of really lame lines (which may also
be found in Marlowe), but the rarity of really fine lines.

The ascriptions to Shakespeare have more historical interst, but
again negative evidence prevails. The title pages of Q2 and Q3, our only
contemporary external evidence, prove nothing. An interregnum quarto The
Excellent Comedy, called The Old Law: Or A new way to please you. By Phil.
Massinger. Tho. Middleton. William Rowley . . . (London: for Edward Archer,
1656), listing "all the Plaies that were ever printed," attributes the

---

[68]Broughton, Gentleman's Magazine, March, 1830, quoted by Tucker Brooke
in "The Marlowe Canon," PMLA, XXXVII (1922), 399.

[69]G. Gregory Smith, "Marlowe and Kyd," in The Cambridge History of English
Literature, ed. A. W. Ward and A. P. Waller (Cambridge: University Press,
1910), V, i, 165.

[70]Marlowe's Imagery and the Marlowe Canon (Philadelphia: University of
Pennsylvania Press, 1940), 199.

[71]Fleay, Biographical Chronicle, II, 65-66.

Raigne to Shakespeare;[72] but "Cymbelona, John of England, Troilus and Cressida and Timon of Athens are entered anonymously," and many apocrypha are assigned to Shakespeare. This list may simply reflect the title pages of Q2 and Q3 or the same unreliable source which supplied the other apocrypha; or it could indicate that the author of the Raigne was unknown, if Shakespeare's King John was listed anonymously because the compiler confused the two versions.

J. O. Halliwell quotes, without approving,[73] Gerard Langbaine's opinion of the two parts (Account of the English Dramatick Poets, 1691): "These plays are not divided into acts, neither are the same with that in folio. I am apt to conjecture that these were first writ by our author, and afterwards revised and reduced into one play by him. . . ." Langbaine's "conjecture" should make us hesitate to suppose with Farmer[74] that some tradition prompted Pope's casual attribution of the Raigne to Shakespeare and "W. Rowley." William Rowley was born about 1585, according to G. E. Bentley, but this date is "a guess derived from the date of publication of his first known work"[75] (1607); since "he was alive in 1624 but dead by 24 March 1625/6" (Bentley, p. 1016), he might have been born early enough to have written the play. But Samuel Rowley was prob-

---

[72]Described by Henrietta C. Bartlett, Mr. William Shakespeare: Original and Early Editions of His Quartos and Folios. His Source Books and Those Containing Contemporary Notices (New Haven, Conn.: Yale University Press; London: Oxford University Press, 1923), p. 181.

[73]Memoranda on Love's Labour's Lost, King John, Othello, and on Romeo and Juliet (London: James Evan Adlard, 1879), p. 83.

[74]Richard Farmer thought that "there must have been some tradition, however erroneous, upon which Mr. Pope's account was founded" (quoted with Pope's note, 1821 Variorum, XV, 193).

[75]The Jacobean and Caroline Stage, 7 vols. (Oxford: Clarendon Press, 1941-1968), V, 1014-1015.

ably at work in the 1590's (Honigmann, p. lv), and Honigmann thinks that he "may have had a hand in the writing" (p. 175). What was Pope's authority for Rowley's name we cannot tell; perhaps "Pope willingly assigned Rowley to Shakespeare as collaborator and whipping-boy."[76] The ascription to Shakespeare is no better grounded, but Edward Capell accepted it: "[The two parts] are but a feeble performance . . . ; notwithstanding, they bear his marks in some places, and in the dying scene strongly."[77] Steevens once thought that the play was Shakespeare's, but later changed his mind.[78] Evidently because of Steevens' _Twenty of the Plays of Shakespeare_, Coleridge included the _Raigne_ in a chronology of Shakespeare's plays,[79] but later he omitted it from similar lists (pp. 211-214).

Ludwig Tieck thought it "ridiculous of the English imprudently to attribute it to . . . anyone else except the one to whom it belongs, because in their opinion it is so wretched and unworthy of the poet [Shakespeare];[80] Rubow remarks that for Tieck "the apocrypha were true Shakespeare. What he sought in Shakespeare, but rarely found, was old-fashioned simplicity. . . . He had reasons for not liking the Renaissance; he strove backward toward the frank, uncomplicated ways of the Middle Ages."[81] A. W. Schlegel thought that Shakespeare's authorship "might probably be made out";[82] and Ulrici agreed at first, though later turning skeptical.[83]

---

[76] Paul V. Rubow, _King John_, p. 11 (my translation).

[77] _Notes and Various Readings to Shakespeare_, 3 vols. (London, 1779-80), I, i, 115.

[78] Charles Knight, _Works of Shakspere_, IV, 230.

[79] _Shakespeare Criticism_, I, 209.

[80] _Alt-Englisches Theater_, I, xvi (my translation).

[81] _King John_, p. 10 (my translation).

[82] _Lectures on Dramatic Art and Literature_, trans. John Black, rev. A. J. W. Morrison (London: Henry G. Bohn, 1846), 446.

[83] _Shakespeare's Dramatic Art_, II, 380.

Few twentieth-century critics have supported the theory. W. J.
Courthope (History of English Poetry, IV, 463-466) is content with arguments which now seem insufficient. A more recent proponent, E. B. Everitt,
makes his claim (and his edition of the play) part of a large scheme for
Shakespeare's early career, to which he assigns several anonymous plays.[84]
Here are his main points: (1) Shakespeare spent the "lost years" as a
lawyer's clerk. (2) His six authentic signatures and "Hand D" in the
additions to Sir Thomas More are that of the hand in the manuscript of
Edmund Ironside (authorial). (3) Edmund Ironside, Leir, and the Raigne,
among other plays, are all Shakespeare's. Each of these points is ques-
tionable: (1) is an hypothesis depending largely on the rest; (2) requires
criteria for handwriting which "exclude much that practical and experi-
enced palaeographers consider to be the basis of the art";[85] and (3)
rests on evidence of doubtful verbal parallels. At best Everitt's
reviewers have been noncommittal.

The Raigne is just not like Shakespeare--in its conventional and
sparse imagery, for example. Yet what he did with his first play makes
fascinating conjecture; unless he sprang to poetic life almost full-grown,
the Raigne might reflect his development about 1587. Temperament is a
further difficulty, however: the heavy-handed polemic of the Raigne seems
clearly the product of another mind. Ulrici calls the monastic scenes
unShakespearean:

The comic element consists merely of bare facts, and these facts are mere
coarse pasquinades. It is in vain to urge that the poet has allowed himself to be carried away by the prevailing popular feeling, and that he

[84]The Young Shakespeare: Studies in Documentary Evidence, Anglistica II,
(Copenhagen: Rosenkilde and Bagger, 1954).

[85]C. J. Sisson, review of The Young Shakespeare in Shakespeare Quarterly,
VI (1955), 456.

has made a sacrifice to popular wit; for in the present case there is no question even of popular wit, and we have abundant proof in Shakespeare's youthful compositions, of how well, even as a young poet, he understood how to make use of true popular wit.[86]

Samuel Johnson provides a broader footing for the argument against Shakespeare: "No man writes upon the same subject twice, without concurring in many places with himself."[87]

The negative evidence besetting all the ascriptions still makes Halliwell's conclusion attractive, that probably "the entire work is the production of one or more authors whose names are yet to be discovered."[88] That alternative is the more disappointing because, as William Watkiss Lloyd says, the Raigne is a good enough play that "the author has good claim for some trouble to be taken to identify him."[89]

V   THE PLAY

1. The Tragedy of King John

Some modern theories of tragedy would exclude the Raigne;[90] renaissance standards and its own profession include it.   In one renaissance

---

[86]Shakespeare's Dramatic Art, II, 380.

[87]The Plays of William Shakespeare, ed. Samuel Johnson, 8 vols. (London: J. and R. Tonson, 1765), III, 504.

[88]Memoranda, p. 80. Whether one author or more than one is uncertain. Dominic rightly concludes that though one author may not have written the whole, a clear case for more than one is impossible because the bulk of the play is homogeneous in style, and the peculiarities of the remainder make ambiguous evidence (pp. 15-19).

[89]Critical Essays on the Plays of Shakespeare (London: George Bell, 1904), p. 190.

[90]In The Origins of English Tragedy (Oxford: Clarendon Press, 1967), p. 122, J. M. R. Margeson remarks: "The various plays that retell the history of King John . . . are . . . sketches of a tragedy that might have been written and never was. No dramatist seems to have been able to work through the historical material of John's reign under the control of a tragic concept to give it concentration and intensity."

view, tragedy recounts the punishment which visits tyranny.[91] So the

rebels' conference (xi.47 ff.) lists the tyrannical acts which justify

John's calling himself "a tragick Tyrant sterne and pitiles" (viii.250);

his lament epitomizes the tyrant's reward (xiii.4-11):

> The world hath wearied me, and I have wearied it:
> It loaths I live, I live and loath my selfe.
> Who pities me? to whom have I been kinde?
> But to a few; a few will pitie me.
> Why dye I not? Death scornes so vilde a pray.
> Why live I not, life hates so sad a prize.
> I sue to both to be retaynd of either,.
> But both are deafe, I can be heard of neither.

He is like the Marlowe hero: "His worship of life gives place to that

craving for death which is the final stage of a false humanism's dialec-

tic."[92] And in "The Tragic Vision of Fulke Greville" Ivor Morris notes:

The evil agencies that mar man's estate, though part of an order as in-
scrutable as it is dark, nevertheless draw part of their being from human
nature. And so they must remain as long as man's primary error—his
'forming his God out of his owne powers'—is perpetuated, for his mis-
placed desire for greatness will lead him to forsake his conscience and
do evil, and his corrupt reason will recommend to him as just, actions
which violate duty and honour.[93]

John's tyranny arises from expediency, as with Arthur (x.49-51):

> Sweete Youth, but that I strived for a Crowne,
> I could have well affoorded to thine age
> Long life, and happines to thy content.

Arthur's accidental death is a consequence of John's murderous intent;

fear for the throne moves him to murder, as he tells Elinor and Hubert

(iv.13-14, 31-33). But why should he fear? He almost invites insubordi-

---

[91]W. A. Armstrong, in "Damon and Pithias and Renaissance Theories of Tragedy," English Studies, XXXIX (1958), 200-201, illustrates this idea with
quotations from Sir Thomas Elyot, Sir Philip Sidney, and Sir John Harington.

[92]M. M. Mahood, Poetry and Humanism (London: Jonathan Cape, 1950), p. 55.

[93]Shakespeare Survey, XIV (1961), 69.

nation when he first defies Pandulph (iii.128-130):

> Mother, come you with me, and for the rest
> That will not follow John in this attempt,
> Confusion light upon their damned soules.

His treatment of Arthur, and the second coronation, seem to expect an imaginary threat; portent and prophecy forbode some "private growing ill / To be inflicted on us in this Clyme" (viii.180-181); fear of Arthur bursts forth when Peter prophesies John's deposition. Why should he behave as a tyrant over unwilling subjects? In delayed exposition at the rebel council, Chester's unjust banishment typifies the barons' "private wrongs" (xi.53); John's tyranny did not begin with Arthur. But the haunting return of his policy with the prince becomes the play's central warning to governors.

"Policy" is the moral norm not only for the King, but for almost everyone in the play. Arthur knows that John "For present vantage would adventure farre" (ii.21), and the compact made before Angiers inspires Shakespeare's Bastard to his famous speech on commodity. Constance "will not sticke to bring [Arthur] to his ende, / So she may bring her selfe to rule a Realme" (i.55-56); Pandulph uses Lewis for the Pope's ends in England; Lewis exploits the English lords, intending to dispatch them; the barons take Arthur's death as pretext for deposing their king.[94] His tragedy is not that of Richard III, who defies society; John instinctively conforms to an immoral world of policy which by rights he should resist.

---

[94]They reject Hubert's retraction of his false account of Arthur's death, though they may see for themselves that the prince has not been blinded, and though they admit that "the murther hath bin newly done, / For yet the body is not fully colde" (ix.79-80). Their real motives come out at St. Edmund's shrine: despite their protestations one feels that but for personal grievances they would not rebel.

His misgivings about expediency begin when it is too late. Blind-

ing Arthur to secure the throne gives the barons excuse to rebel, but

eventually no course is expedient (viii.241-242):

> His life a foe that leveld at my crowne,
> His death a frame to pull my building downe.

At his death John reveals a moral and spiritual sense hitherto unseen

(xv.66-68, 74-75, 82-85):

> Me thinks I see a cattalogue of sinne
> Wrote by a fiend in Marble characters,
> The least enough to loose my part in heaven.
> .   .   .   .   .   .
> And there is none so mercifull a God
> That will forgive the number of my sinnes.
> .   .   .   .   .   .
> My life repleat with rage and tyranie,
> Craves little pittie for so strange a death.
> Or who will say that John disceasd too soone,
> Who will not say he rather livd too long.

This new note is plausible; Melun's death prepares us for such an about-

face--his qualms at death (xii.113-115) emphasize how one may temporarily

ignore spiritual values to embrace expediency. Like Melun, John repudi-

ates his worldly career in the face of death--which brings home to him

his failure by both worldly and divine standards. The tyrant's isolation

and defeat invites pity; personal weakness prevents him from finishing

his greatest labor: emancipating England from Rome. Ironically the

popelings' malice, not John's sin, causes his death.

John is more than a warning to tyrants; he is a victim of papal

aggression and a precursor of protestant reform. His nemesis is peculiar:

this play transcends the de casibus tradition;[95] yet the king's death is

[95]Willard Farnham observes in The Medieval Heritage of Elizabethan Tragedy,
rev. ed. (Oxford: University Press, 1950), p. 406, that "those in the play
who suffer reverses suffer them without cursing any such easily blameable
figure of fate" as the medieval Fortune.

not due to any deed of his which the author would reprehend. Arthur

plagues his conscience, but John dies of poison because he contemned the

church of Rome. The tyrant-martyr is a singular tragic hero--suffering

for his sins, but dying for good deeds. The moral is clear: unchecked

the church of Rome destroys what it cannot control. J. L. Simmons finds

here a fatal flaw:

The moral value which has been placed upon the papal conflict, as well
as upon the supporting anti-papist antics, is extraneous and jarring; it
ruins the play not because one should be broadminded about Roman Catholics but because it is irrelevant to the genuinely dramatic moral vision.[96]

Is the <u>Raigne</u> hopelessly divided between contradictory views of John

as tyrant and martyr, and between mutually exclusive purposes of tragedy

and politics? Rather the dramatist has subordinated tyrant-tragedy to

martyr-history. The key is the king's last speech (xv.95-110):

> Since John did yeeld unto the Priest of <u>Rome,</u>
> Nor he nor his have prospred on the earth:
> Curst are his blessings, and his curse is blisse.
> But in the spirit I cry unto my God,
> As did the Kingly Prophet <u>David</u> cry,
> (Whose hands, as mine, with murder were attaint)
> I am not he shall buyld the Lord a house,
> Or roote these Locusts from the face of earth:
> But if my dying heart deceave me not,
> From out these loynes shall spring a Kingly braunch
> Whose armes shall reach unto the gates of <u>Rome,</u>
> And with his feete treade downe the Strumpets pride,
> That sits upon the chaire of <u>Babylon.</u>
> <u>Philip,</u> my heart strings breake, the poysons flame
> Hath overcome in me weake Natures power,
> And in the faith of Jesu <u>John</u> doth dye.

Now God accepted David's repentance; yet he was disqualified from

building the temple. So John's contrition ensures his salvation though

he cannot conquer papal tyranny; emancipation from Rome must be begun by

Henry VIII and ratified by Elizabeth and her subjects. The dramatist in-

vites his audience to help maintain their precarious freedom through

[96]"Shakespeare's <u>King John</u> and Its Source," 57.

loyalty to Elizabeth; King John's tragic end clinches the Elizabethan
themes of politics and religion which are the purpose of the play.

2. The History of King John

The play has two obvious historical functions: King John's career
exemplifies the course that Elizabethans should pursue in 1591; his death
and unfinished work become a cause for the spectators. On one hand the
play represents the reign of John as a parallel to Elizabethan conditions; on the other, English emancipation from Rome is represented as the
culmination of the great enterprise which King John began.

Much of the force of The Troublesome Raigne depends on the spectators' seeing their own political and religious situation in the scene
before them. At first Elizabeth had tried to allow Catholics private
freedom of conscience in return for outward conformity and patriotism;
the queen wished her subjects not to be forced to an explicit choice
between two masters, and this policy proved feasible during the first
decade of her reign. But when Pope Pius V finally issued a bull, published in England in 1570, excommunicating and deposing the Queen and
calling upon English Catholics to repudiate her as a heretic, religion
and politics became inextricable. Once the Pope clearly demonstrated
the contradiction of double loyalty, staunch English papists could
scarcely avoid the imputation of treason. The instructions of Cardinal
Morone in 1579 "show that the object of the papal court was to allow
the English Romanists to obtain all the advantages of seeming to be
loyal to Elizabeth while at the same time they were to put her to death
if possible, and to rise against her if there were a reasonable chance
of success."[97] The government may have made propaganda by conniving in

[97]M. Petriburg, "The Excommunication of Queen Elizabeth," English Historical Review, VII (1892), 82.

some of the ensuing plots, but other attempts on the Queen's life cer-

tainly depended on genuine zeal for Rome; and if the Armada had been able

to implement the papal deposition, England would have passed into the

Spanish sphere of influence. (See Appendix for the bull of the Armada.)

The Troublesome Raigne reproduces most of these particulars. Pan-

dulph's sentence specifically charges the English to murder their king;

the monkish murderer hopes to be canonized for his deed. John's recon-

ciliation with Rome reminds Elizabethans that the Pope claims complete

temporal authority: the offers of submission on John's terms (x.181-187)

are flatly refused; when he surrenders unconditionally Pandulph receives

him as vassal of the Pope. The French make duty to Rome a pretext for

aggrandizement in England. At the rebel council the Bastard echoes the

"Homily Against Disobedience and Wilful Rebellion" required to be heard

in church at frequent intervals. The Franciscan friars mirror a fact

reiterated in England--that Sixtus V, the pope who blessed the Armada,

was a Franciscan. A provision of the Act of Supremacy (1559)[98] turns up

in John's resolve (iv.21-25):

> And whatsoere he be within my Land,
> That goes to Rome for justice and for law,
> While he may have his right within the Realme,
> Let him be judgde a traitor to the State,
> And suffer as an enemie to England.

The dangerous tendency of Peter's prophecies might suggest the year 1570,

when "the papists were full of confident expectations of their golden day,

as they termed it: and divers wizards predicted strange things in their

[98]"No foreign prince, person, prelate, state or potentate, spiritual or
temporal, shall at any time after the last day of this session of Parlia-
ment, use, enjoy or exercise any manner of power, jurisdiction, superiority,
authority, preeminence or privilege, spiritual or ecclesiastical, within
this realm . . ." (1 Eliz. l.vii).

behalf."[99] The precedent of John's troublesome reign emphasizes the duty

of loyal vigilance against religious and political subversion.

If this analogue were the only kind of political and religious

commentary in the play it might more plausibly be called "tiresomely

didactic."[100] But the sense of historical continuity must have appealed

strongly to the contemporary imagination: John's task of liberating

England is left unfinished, but his dying prophecy extends the main

enterprise of the play to the time of the Tudors; now, in 1591, his

greatest objective has been realized, but it is up to Englishmen to

maintain the liberty of English church and state. The audience is

invited to ensure that John's suffering and martyrdom shall not have

been futile, by acting on the good advice implicit in the historical

parallels; for Elizabethan protestants the play creates an irresist-

ible sense of solidarity with King John. Since the matter of the play

thus comes home to men's business and bosoms it may be didactic, but

hardly tiresome. That such propaganda was both useful and popular is

evident from the extent of the tradition of public demonstrations in

England against popery. According to Sydney Anglo, in 1533 the Privy

Council "discussed the necessity of having sermons preached throughout

the country against the authority of the Pope";[101] Thomas Cromwell

encouraged John Bale and others to write pamphlets and drama as anti-

Roman propaganda in the thirties; and "bonfires and processions . . .

[99] John Strype, _Annals of the Reformation_ . . . _during Queen Elizabeth's Happy Reign_, new ed. 4 vols. (Oxford, 1824), I, ii, 354.

[100] A. P. Rossiter, ed., "Preface. II. Morals and Histories," _Woodstock: A Moral History_ (London: Chatto and Windus, 1946), p. 7.

[101] "An Early Tudor Programme for Plays and Other Demonstrations Against the Pope," _Journal of the Warburg and Courtauld Institutes_, XX (1957), 177.

were already a feature of the campaign against images in 1538, while by June of the following year a foreign observer was led to remark that every village feast or pastime included sports and follies against the Pope." After 1558 Accession Day became a "national festival" of "prayers and sermons, bell-ringing, bonfires and feasting"[102] celebrating Elizabeth's government, but also commemorating England's final separation from Rome.

The Troublesome Raigne is one of many propaganda pieces written in those especially anxious years just before and after the Armada. Like many of them it comments on current events by making clear and obvious historical analogues; but it also invites the Elizabethan audience to help resolve the conflict in which King John was martyred.

3. The Romance of King Richard's Son

Because Elizabethans knew that King John was not a good king, the dramatist took special pains to qualify him as hero-martyr by borrowing the aura of Richard I, who shared with Henry V the greatest honor accorded by Elizabethans to any English heroes. John could interest Elizabethans simply by being Richard's brother. But in the Raigne he gains much more prestige from the electric atmosphere surrounding the reincarnation of Richard in Philip the Bastard. On their first meeting John declares: "In my life / I never saw so lively counterfet / Of Richard Cordelion, as in him" (i.193-195). Englishmen in the sixteenth century would not share our difficulties with the proportion of space devoted to the Bastard early in the play; the longer the expatiation on Philip's

---

[102] Roy C. Strong, "The Popular Celebration of the Accession Day of Queen Elizabeth I," Journal of the Warburg and Courtauld Institutes, XXI (1958), 87.

character and exploits the more their gratification: Richard's glories,
once cut off by his untimely death, are now revived in a lost son. Had
the Bastard been quite irrelevant to the main action they would still
have justified dragging Richard into a play about John, as nineteenth-
century Englishmen could approve Beerbohm Tree's introduction of the
Magna Carta to Shakespeare's King John. Hence Philip's prominence on
the title page: "The Troublesome Raigne of John King of England, with
the discoverie of King Richard Cordelions Base sonne (vulgarly named,
the Bastard Fawconbridge)."

Thus the reader is treated to the spectacle of Philip renouncing
goods and land for the glory of his bastardy, and proving himself wor-
thy of his father. Shakespeare was apparently not so concerned to ex-
ploit Richard's memory: he omits Philip's trance and preternatural
intimations of royalty, and generally lays less emphasis on the Bastard's part except where he contributes directly to the main action and
themes. But Elizabethans must have delighted in his long internal
deliberation over his paternity and his determination to make his
mother corroborate his own divinings.

The author obliges his audience with vengeance upon the slayer of
King Richard in several separate encounters with Philip. Limoges'
boasting of "Richards pride, and Richards fall" inspires the Bastard's
first threat--gloriously heroic though bombastic (ii.135-136, 152-158):

> What words are these? how doo my sinews shake?
> My Fathers foe clad in my Fathers spoyle.
> .   .   .   .
> But arme thee traytor, wronger of renowme,
> For by his soule I sweare, my Fathers soule,
> Twice will I not review the Mornings rise,
> Till I have torne that Trophei from thy back,
> And split thy heart, for wearing it so long.
> Philip hath sworne, and if it be not done,
> Let not the world repute me Richards Sonne.

When the Bastard recaptures the lionskin and challenges Limoges to single combat, the enemy's cowardice not only reassures us that Richard's death was a fluke, but also underscores Philip's valor. Queen Elinor exclaims (iii.59-60): "Thy forwardnes this day hath joyd my soule, / And made me thinke my Richard lives in thee." Finally the Bastard avenges his father's death in the battle begun at Pandulph's instigation (iii.146-158):

> Thus hath K. Richards Sonne performde his vowes.
> And offred Austrias bloud for sacrifice
> Unto his fathers everliving soule.
> Brave Cordelion, now my heart doth say,
> I have deservde, though not to be thy heire
> Yet as I am, thy base begotten sonne,
> A name as pleasing to thy Philips heart,
> As to be cald the Duke of Normandie.
> Lie there a pray to every ravening fowle:
> And as my Father triumpht in thy spoyles,
> And trode thine Ensignes underneath his feete,
> So doo I tread upon thy cursed selfe,
> And leave thy bodie to the fowles for food.

Philip dominates the beginning scene, and captures a good deal of the attention in two further scenes which, with the first, comprise more than a third of the play.

Limoges is superfluous to the main plot. The dramatist uses him to develop the story of Richard's son and to clarify issues early in the play. The first speech uttered before Angiers identifies one of Arthur's supporters as "Brave Austria, cause of Cordelions death" (ii. 4); by irresistible association Arthur's party becomes "the enemy." The potential for divided loyalties in John's struggle with Arthur may indeed have been "the chief element in its appeal to Shakespeare"[103] if he found it in the Raigne--he begins by making John a usurper. But the anonymous author simply does not emphasize divided loyalties: thematic con-

---

[103]Michael Manheim, The Weak King Dilemma in the Shakespearean History Play (Syracuse, N.Y.: Syracuse University Press, 1973), p. 129. The quotation following is from the same place.

cerns seem rather to have led him to simplify the issues (Gary, pp. 74–79). Richard's slayer is an important means to this end: Elizabethans could hardly refuse the argumentum ad hominem which taints Arthur's cause from the first.

If Limoges serves to make the bad of an historically ambiguous situation worse, Philip does much more to make the good better. In the first third of the play he gratifies special expectations tangential to the main action; but the enthusiasm thus engendered helps maintain sympathy for King John throughout. Just putting Richard's son in John's camp is a good beginning; later Philip exemplifies rightful loyalty to John when the barons are deluded into rebellion. Doubtful hero that he is, John needs all the enhancement possible: not all readers can accept the play's simplified versions of right and wrong. Manheim says:

In TR loyalties are severely divided, culminating in that ultimate division in the audience between king and conscience. Nothing is resolved by the last scene, really. The Bastard may speak of England being true to itself, but wherein lies that being true? In fealty to a child-murderer usurper? The nobles were wrong to defect to France, but their motives seemed justified. There seemed little alternative at the time. In retrospect, they were countenancing Arthur's death by remaining loyal, John's death by defecting. They are damned both ways. The ending brings the deus ex machina in the form of the successor. But this resolves nothing. The contradictory feelings of the weak-king plays seem nowhere more deadlocked than in TR.

But only Shakespeare's Bastard feels these conflicts; over Arthur's corpse he tells Hubert (IV.iii.140–147):

> I am amaz'd, methinks, and lose my way
> Among the thorns and dangers of this world.
> How easy dost thou take all England up
> From forth this morsel of dead royalty!
> The life, the right and truth of all this realm
> Is fled to heaven; and England now is left
> To tug and scamble, and to part by th' teeth
> The unow'd interest of proud swelling state.

The Raigne diverts us from these complexities, bringing to John's cause the full support of Philip with all the prestige of his birth and exploits.

The Bastard's conflicts with Limoges receive much more extensive treatment than in Shakespeare; Philip effects the plunder of the abbeys in a
special scene; and he defends the king to the revolted nobles in a long
speech which has no counterpart in Shakespeare, and which reduces the
issues to stark simplicity (xi.108-109, 117-122):

> For Arthurs death King John was innocent,
> He desperat was the deathsman to himselfe.
> .   .   .   .   .   .
> Why Salsburie admit the wrongs are true,
> Yet subjects may not take in hand revenge,
> And rob the heavens of their proper power,
> Where sitteth he to whome revenge belongs.
> And doth a Pope, a Priest, a man of pride
> Give charters for the lives of lawfull Kings?

England's being true to itself lies in fealty to John; in the Raigne
as in history he is not a usurper, and for the Bastard he is not a
child-murderer. Unlike Shakespeare, the anonymous author invokes the
reflected glory of Richard until the end of the play; with some imaginative effort we can appreciate how Elizabethans must have responded to
the Bastard's exhortation (xii.80-87):

> Betake your self to armes, my troupes are prest
> To answere Lewes with a lustie shocke:
> The English Archers have their quivers full,
> Their bowes are bent, the pykes are prest to push:
> God cheere my Lord, K. Richards fortune hangs
> Upon the plume of warlike Philips helme.
> Then let them know his brother and his sonne
> Are leaders of the Englishmen at armes.

For the final appeal, that "Englands Peeres and people joyne in one,"
the Bastard is not just a convenient spokesman, but the son of Richard.

   To emphasize conflicting claims for loyalty in The Troublesome
Raigne is surely to confuse the play with what we find embedded in the
prose histories and exploited in King John after Shakespeare's charac-
teristic manner. To those who had ears to hear, Shakespeare offered a

complex world; but we cannot conclude that all Elizabethans were impatient with the simplistic contrasts of the _Raigne_. This propaganda piece redeems an unpromising hero partly by treating him tragically, and partly by infusing the atmosphere with the glory of Richard I.

THE TROUBLESOME RAIGNE OF JOHN KING OF ENGLAND

DRAMATIS PERSONAE

John, King of England

Elinor, mother to King John

William Marshal, Earl of Pembrooke

Thomas Plantaginet, Earl of Salisbury

The Earl of Essex

Chattilion, the French ambassador

Thomas Nidigate, the Sheriff of Northamptonshire

Margaret, Lady Fauconbridge, widow to Sir Robert Fauconbridge

Robert Fauconbridge, son to Sir Robert

Philip Fauconbridge, bastard son to King Richard I by Lady
    Margaret

Philip, King of France

Lewes, son to King Philip

Lymoges, Duke of Austria

Constance, widow to Geoffrey, Duke of Brittany

Arthur, Duke of Brittany and son to Geoffrey

Blanch, daughter to Alphonso VIII (King of Spain) and Elinor
    (daughter to Henry II of England and Queen Elinor)

A citizen of Angiers

English Herald

French Herald

Pandulph, Cardinal of Milan and papal legate

Hubert de Burgh

Thomas, Anthony, and Laurence, Franciscan friars

Alice, a nun

Peter, a prophet of Pomfret

A boy

Three attendants to Hubert de Burgh

The Earl of Bewchampe

The Earl of Percy

The Viscount Melun

A French lord

The abbot of Swinstead Abbey

Thomas, a monk of Swinstead

Two friars of Swinstead

Henry, son to King John and afterwards King Henry III of
    England

Messengers

Citizens of Angiers, Townspeople, English Nobles, Bishops,
    Priests, French lords, Monks of Swinstead, Attendants

THE

Troublesome Raigne

of John King of England, with the dis-

coverie of King Richard Cordelions

Base sonne (vulgarly named, The Ba-

stard Fawconbridge): also the

death of King John at Swinstead

Abbey.

As it was (sundry times) publikely acted by the

Queenes Majesties Players, in the ho-

nourable Citie of

London.

[device]

Imprinted at London for Sampson Clarke,

and are to be solde at his shop, on the backe-

side of the Royall Exchange.

1591.

4

To the Gentlemen Readers.   IA2

You that with friendly grace of smoothed brow
Have entertaind the <u>Scythian</u> <u>Tamburlaine,</u>
And given applause unto an Infidel:
Vouchsafe to welcome (with like curtesie)
A warlike Christian and your Countreyman.   5
For Christs true faith indur'd he many a storme,
And set himselfe against the Man of <u>Rome,</u>
Untill base treason (by a damned wight)
Did all his former triumphs put to flight,
Accept of it (sweete Gentles) in good sort,   10
And thinke it was preparde for your disport.

The troublesome Raigne of

<u>King</u> <u>John</u>.

Scene i

<u>Enter</u> <u>K</u>. John, <u>Queene</u> Elinor <u>his</u> <u>mother,</u> William Marshal

<u>Earle</u> <u>of</u> Pembrooke, <u>the</u> <u>Earles</u> <u>of</u> Essex, <u>and</u> <u>of</u> Salisbury.

<u>Elinor</u>

Barons of <u>England</u>, and my noble Lords;

Though God and Fortune have bereft from us

Victorious <u>Richard</u> scourge of Infidels,

And clad this Land in stole of dismall hieu:

Yet give me leave to joy, and joy you all,   5

That from this wombe hath sprung a second hope,

A King that may in rule and vertue both

Succeede his brother in his Emperie.

K. John

    My gracious mother Queene, and Barons all;

    Though farre unworthie of so high a place,   10

    As is the Throne of mightie Englands King:

    Yet John your Lord, contented uncontent,

    Will (as he may) sustaine the heavie yoke

    Of pressing cares, that hang upon a Crowne.

    My Lord of Pembrooke and Lord Salsbury,   15

    Admit the Lord Shattilion to our presence;

    That we may know what Philip King of Fraunce

    (By his Ambassadors) requires of us.

                    Exeunt Pembrooke and Salisbury.

Elinor

    Dare lay my hand that Elinor can gesse

    Whereto this weightie Embassade doth tend: 20

    If of my Nephew Arthur and his claime,

    Then say my Sonne I have not mist my aime.

Enter Chattilion and the two Earles.   IA3^v

K. John

My Lord Chattilion, welcome into England:

How fares our Brother Philip King of Fraunce?

Chattilion

His Highnes at my comming was in health,   25

And wild me to salute your Majestie,

And say the message he hath given in charge.

K. John

And spare not man, we are preparde to heare.

Chattilion

Philip by the grace of God most Christian K. of France,

having taken into his guardain and protection Arthur   30

Duke of Brittaine, son and heire to Jeffrey thine elder

brother, requireth in the behalfe of the said Arthur, the

Kingdom of England, with the Lordship of Ireland, Poiters,

Anjow, Torain, Main: and I attend thine aunswere.

K. John

A small request: belike he makes account   35

That England, Ireland, Poiters, Anjow, Torain, Main,

Are nothing for a King to give at once:

I wonder what he meanes to leave for me.

Tell Philip, he may keepe his Lords at home,

With greater honour than to send them thus   40

On Embassades that not concerne himselfe,

Or if they did, would yeeld but small returne.

Chattilion

Is this thine answere?

K. John

It is, and too good an answer for so proud a message.

Chattilion

Then King of England, in my Masters name,   45

And in Prince Arthur Duke of Britaines name,

I doo defie thee as an Enemie,

And wish thee to prepare for bloodie warres.

Elinor

My Lord (that stands upon defiance thus)

Commend me to my Nephew, tell the boy,   50

That I Queene Elianor (his Grandmother)

Upon my blessing charge him leave his Armes,

Whereto his head-strong Mother pricks him so:

Her pride we know, and know her for a Dame

That will not sticke to bring him to his ende,   55

So she may bring her selfe to rule a Realme.

Next wish him to forsake the King of Fraunce,

And come to me and to his Unckle here,   IA4
And he shall want for nothing at our hands.
<u>Chattilion</u>
This shall I doo, and thus I take my leave.   60
<u>K</u>. <u>John</u>
<u>Pembrooke</u>, convay him safely to the sea,
But not in hast: for as we are advisde,
We meane to be in <u>Fraunce</u> as soone as he,
To fortefie such townes as we possesse
In <u>Anjou</u>, <u>Torain</u> and in <u>Normandy</u>.   65

                    <u>Exeunt</u> Chattilion <u>and</u> Pembrooke.
<u>Enter</u> <u>the</u> <u>Shrive</u>, Thomas Nidigate, <u>with</u> Margaret, <u>Lady</u>
Fauconbridge <u>and</u> <u>her</u> <u>sons</u> Robert <u>and</u> Philip <u>the</u> <u>Bastard</u>,
<u>and</u> <u>whispers</u> <u>the</u> <u>Earle</u> <u>of</u> Sals <u>in</u> <u>the</u> <u>eare</u>.
<u>Salisbury</u>
Please it your Majestie, heere is the Shrive of <u>Northhamp-</u>
<u>tonshire</u>, with certaine persons that of late committed a
riot, and have appeald to your Majestie beseeching your
Highnes for speciall cause to heare them.
<u>K</u>. <u>John</u>
Wil them come neere, and while we heare the cause,   70
Goe <u>Salsbury</u> and make provision,
We meane with speede to passe the sea to <u>Fraunce</u>.

                              <u>Exit</u> Salisbury.
Say Shrieve, what are these men, what have they done?
Or wheretoo tends the course of this appeale?

Thomas

Please it your Majestie these two brethren unnaturally 75
falling at odds about their Fathers living have broken
your Highnes peace, in seeking to right their own wrongs
without cause of Law, or order of Justice, and unlawfully
assembled themselves in mutinous manner, having committed
a riot, appealing from triall in their Countrey to   80
your Highnes: and here I <u>Thomas</u> <u>Nidigate</u> Shrieve of <u>North-</u>
<u>hamptonshire</u>, doo deliver them over to their triall.

<u>K.</u> <u>John</u>

My Lord of <u>Essex</u>, will the offenders to stand foorth, and
tell the cause of their quarrell.

Essex

Gentlemen, it is the Kings pleasure that you discover   85
your griefes, and doubt not but you shall have justice.

Bastard

Please it your Majestie, the wrong is mine; yet wil I
abide all wrongs, before I once open my mouth to unrippe
the shamefull slaunder of my parents, the dishonour of
myself, and the wicked dealing of my brother in this   90
princely assembly.

Robert

Then by my Prince his leave shall <u>Robert</u> speake,
And tell your Majestie what right I have

To offer wrong, as he accounteth wrong.   IA4^V

My Father (not unknowen unto your Grace)   95

Receivd his spurres of Knighthood in the Field,

At Kingly Richards hands in Palestine,

When as the walls of Acon gave him way:

His name Sir Robert Fauconbridge of Mountbery.

What by succession from his Auncestours,   100

And warlike service under Englands Armes,

His living did amount too at his death

Two thousand Markes revenew every yeare:

And this (my Lord) I challenge for my right,

As lawfull heire to Robert Fauconbridge.   105

Bastard

If first-borne sonne be heire indubitate

By certaine right of Englands auncient Lawe,

How should myselfe make any other doubt,

But I am heire to Robert Fauconbridge?

K. John

Fond Youth, to trouble these our Princely eares   110

Or make a question in so plaine a case:

Speake, is this man thine elder Brother borne?

Robert

    Please it your Grace with patience for to heare;

    I not denie but he mine Elder is,

    Mine elder Brother too: yet in such sort,   115

    As he can make no title to the Land.

K. John

    A doubtfull tale as ever I did heare,

    Thy Brother and thine elder, and no heire:

    Explaine this darke Aenigma.

Robert

    I graunt (my Lord) he is my mothers sonne,   120

    Base borne, and base begot, no Fauconbridge.

    Indeede the world reputes him lawfull heire,

    My Father in his life did count him so,

    And here my Mother stands to proove him so:

    But I (my Lord) can proove, and doo averre   125

    Both to my Mothers shame and his reproach,

    He is no heire, nor yet legitimate.

    Then (gracious Lord) let Fauconbridge enjoy

    The living that belongs to Fauconbridge.

And let not him possesse anothers right.   IB1   130

K. John

Prove this, the land is thine by Englands law.

Elinor

Ungracious youth, to rip thy mothers shame,

The wombe from whence thou didst thy being take,

All honest eares abhorre thy wickednes,

But gold I see doth beate downe natures law.   135

Margaret

My gracious Lord, and you thrice reverend Dame,

That see the teares distilling from mine eyes,

And scalding sighes blowne from a rented heart:

For honour and regard of womanhood,

Let me entreate to be commaunded hence.   140

Let not these eares receive the hissing sound

Of such a viper, who with poysoned words

Doth masserate the bowels of my soule.

K. John

Ladie, stand up, be patient for a while:

And fellow, say, whose bastard is thy brother.   145

Bastard

Not for my selfe, nor for my mother now:

But for the honour of so brave a Man,

Whom he accuseth with adulterie:

Here I beseech your Grace upon my knees,

To count him mad, and so dismisse us hence.   150

Robert

Nor mad, nor mazde, but well advised, I

Charge thee before this royall presence here

To be a Bastard to King Richards self,

Sonne to your Grace, and Brother to your Majestie.

Thus bluntly, and--   155

Elinor

Yong man:

Thou needst not be ashamed of thy kin,

Nor of thy Sire. But forward with thy proofe.

Robert

The proofe so plaine, the argument so strong,

As that your Highnes and these noble Lords,   160

And all (save those that have no eyes to see)

Shall sweare him to be Bastard to the King.

First when my Father was Embassadour

In Germanie unto the Emperour,

The King lay often at my Fathers house;   165

And all the Realme suspected what befell:

And at my Fathers back returne agen   IB1^v

My Mother was delivered as tis sed,

Sixe weekes before the account my Father made.

But more than this: looke but on Philips face,   170

His features, actions, and his lineaments,

And all this Princely presence shall confesse,

He is no other but King Richards Sonne.

Then gracious Lord, rest he King Richards Sonne,

And let me rest safe in my Fathers right,   175

That am his rightfull sonne and onely heire.

K. John

Is this thy proofe, and all thou hast to say?

Robert

I have no more, nor neede I greater proofe.

K. John

First, where thou saidst in absence of thy Sire

My Brother often lodged in his house: 180

And what of that? base groome to slaunder him,

That honoured his Embassador so much,

In absence of the man to cheere the wife?

This will not hold, proceede unto the next.

Elinor

    Thou saist she teemde six weeks before her time.   185

    Why good Sir Squire are you so cunning growen

    To make account of womens reckonings:

    Spit in your hand and to your other proofes:

    Many mischaunces hap in such affaires

    To make a woman come before her time.   190

K. John

    And where thou saist he looketh like the King

    In action, feature and proportion:

    Therein I holde with thee, for in my life

    I never saw so lively counterfet

    Of Richard Cordelion, as in him.   195

Robert

    Then good my Lord, be you indifferent Judge,

    And let me have my living and my right.

Elinor

    Nay heare you Sir, you runne away too fast:

    Know you not, Omne simile non est idem?

    Or have read in. Harke ye good sir,   200

    Twas thus I warrant, and no otherwise,

    She lay with Sir Robert your Father, and thought uppon

King <u>Richard</u> my Sonne, and so your Brother was   IB2

formed in this fashion.

<u>Robert</u>

Madame, you wrong me thus to jest it out,   205

I crave my right: King <u>John</u> as thou are King,

So be thou just, and let me have my right.

<u>K</u>. John

Why (foolish boy) thy proofes are frivolous,

Nor canst thou chalenge any thing thereby.

But thou shalt see how I will helpe thy claime,   210

This is my doome, and this my doome shall stand

Irrevocable, as I am King of <u>England</u>.

For thou knowst not, weele aske of them that know,

His mother and himselfe shall ende this strife:

And as they say, so shall thy living passe.   215

<u>Robert</u>

My Lord, herein I chalenge you of wrong,

To give away my right, and put the doome

Unto themselves. Can there be likelihood

That she will loose?

Or he will give the living from himselfe?   220

It may not be my Lord. Why should it be?

<u>K</u>. John

Lords keepe him back, and let him heare the doome.

<u>Essex</u>,

First aske the Mother thrice who was his Sire?

Essex

    Ladie Margaret Widow of Fauconbridge,   225

    Who was Father to thy Sonne Philip?

Margaret

    Please it your Majestie, Sir Robert Fauconbridge.

Robert

    This is right, aske my felow there if I be a thiefe.

K. John

    Aske Philip whose Sonne he is.

Essex

    Philip, who was thy Father?   230

Bastard

    Mas my Lord, and thats a question: and you had not

    taken some paines with her before, I should have

    desired you to aske my Mother.

K. John

    Say who was thy Father?

Bastard

    Faith (my Lord) to answere you sure he is my father   235

    that was neerest my mother when I was gotten, and

    him I thinke to be Sir Robert Fauconbridge.

K. John

    Essex, for fashions sake demaund agen,

    And so an ende to this contention.

<u>Robert</u>   IB2^{V}

 Was ever man thus wrongd as <u>Robert</u> is?   240

<u>Essex</u>

 <u>Philip</u> speake I say, who was thy Father?

<u>K. John</u>

 Yong man how now, what art thou in a traunce?

<u>Elinor</u>

 <u>Philip</u> awake,--The man is in a dreame.

<u>Bastard</u>

 --<u>Philippus atavis</u> aedite <u>Regibus</u>.

 What saist thou <u>Philip?</u> Sprung of auncient Kings?   245

 <u>Quo me rapit tempestas?</u>

 What winde of honour blowes this furie forth?

 Or whence proceede these fumes of Majestie?

 Me thinkes I heare a hollow Eccho sound,

 That <u>Philip</u> is the Sonne unto a King: 250

 The whistling leaves upon the trembling trees,

 Whistle in consort I am <u>Richards</u> Sonne:

 The bubling murmur of the waters fall,

 Records <u>Philippus Regis filius</u>:

 Birds in their flight make musicke with their wings,   255

 Filling the ayre with glorie of my birth:

Birds, bubbles, leaves, and mountaines Eccho, all

Ring in mine eares, that I am <u>Richards</u> Sonne.

Fond man, ah whether art thou carried?

How are thy thoughts ywrapt in Honors heaven?   260

Forgetfull what thou art, and whence thou camst.

Thy Fathers land cannot maintaine these thoughts,

These thoughts are farre unfitting <u>Fauconbridge</u>:

And well they may; for why this mounting minde

Doth soare too high to stoupe to <u>Fauconbridge</u>.   265

Why how now? knowest thou where thou art?

And knowest thou who expects thine answere here?

Wilt thou upon a frantick madding vaine

Goe loose thy land, and say thy selfe base borne?

No, keepe thy land, though <u>Richard</u> were thy Sire,   270

What ere thou thinkst, say thou art <u>Fauconbridge</u>.--

<u>K</u>. <u>John</u>

Speake man, be sodaine, who thy Father was.

<u>Bastard</u>

Please it your Majestie, Sir <u>Robert</u>--

<u>Philip</u>, that <u>Fauconbridge</u> cleaves to thy jawes:

It will not out, I cannot for my life   275

Say I am Sonne unto a Fauconbridge.   IB3

Let land and living goe, tis honors fire

That makes me sweare King Richard was my Sire.

Base to a King addes title of more State,

Than Knights begotten, though legittimate.--   280

Please it your Grace, I am King Richards Sonne.

Robert

    Robert revive thy heart, let sorrow die,

    His faltring tongue not suffers him to lie.

Margaret

    What head-strong furie doth enchaunt my sonne?

Bastard

    Philip cannot repent, for he hath done.   285

K. John

    Then Philip blame not me, thy selfe hast lost

    By wilfulnesse, thy living and thy land.

    Robert, thou art the heire of Fauconbridge,

    God give thee joy, greater than thy desert.

Elinor

    Why how now Philip, give away thine owne?   290

Bastard

    Madame, I am bold to make my selfe your nephew,

    The poorest kinsman that your Highnes hath:

And with this Proverb gin the world anew,

Help hands, I have no lands, honour is my desire;

Let <u>Philip</u> live to shew himselfe worthie so great   295

    a Sire.

<u>Elinor</u>

<u>Philip</u>, I think thou knewst thy Grandams minde:

But cheere thee boy, I will not see thee want

As long as <u>Elinor</u> hath foote of land;

Henceforth thou shalt be taken for my sonne,

And waite on me and on thine Unckle heere,   300

Who shall give honour to thy noble minde.

<u>K. John</u>

<u>Philip</u> kneele down, that thou maist throughly know

How much thy resolution pleaseth us,

Rise up Sir <u>Richard Plantaginet</u> K. <u>Richards</u> Sonne.

<u>Bastard</u>

Graunt heavens that <u>Philip</u> once may shew himself   305

Worthie the honour of <u>Plantaginet</u>,

Or basest glorie of a Bastards name.

<u>K. John</u>

Now Gentlemen, we will away to <u>France</u>,

To checke the pride of <u>Arthur</u> and his mates:

<u>Essex</u>, thou shalt be Ruler of my Realme,   310

And toward the maine charges of my warres,

Ile ceaze the lazie Abbey lubbers lands   IB3^v

Into my hands to pay my men of warre.

The Pope and Popelings shall not grease themselves

With golde and groates, that are the souldiers due.   315

Thus forward Lords, let our commaund be done,

And march we forward mightely to <u>Fraunce</u>.   <u>Exeunt</u>.

<u>Manent</u> Philip <u>and</u> <u>his</u> <u>Mother</u>.

Bastard

Madame I beseech you deigne me so much leasure as

the hearing of a matter that I long to impart to you.

Margaret

Whats the matter <u>Philip,</u> I thinke your sute in   320

secret, tends to some money matter, which you

suppose burns in the bottome of my chest.

Bastard

No Madam,

It is no such sute as to beg or borrow,

But such a sute, as might some other grant,   325

I would not now have troubled you withall.

Margaret

A Gods name let us heare it.

Bastard

    Then Madame thus, your Ladiship sees well,

    How that my scandall growes by meanes of you,

    In that report hath rumord up and downe,   330

    I am a bastard, and no Fauconbridge.

    This grose attaint so tilteth in my thoughts,

    Maintaining combat to abridge my ease,

    That field and towne, company and alone,

    Whatso I doo, or wheresoere I am,   335

    I cannot chase the slaunder from my thoughts.

    If it be true, resolve me of my Sire,

    For pardon Madame, if I thinke amisse.

    Be Philip Philip and no Fauconbridge,

    His Father doubtles was as brave a man.   340

    To you on knees as sometime Phaeton,

    Mistrusting silly Merop for his Sire,

    Strayning a little bashfull modestie,

    I beg some instance whence I am extraught.

Margaret

    Yet more adoo to haste me to my grave,   345

    And wilt thou too become a Mothers crosse?

    Must I accuse myself to close with you?

Slaunder myself to quiet your affects: IB4

Thou moovst me <u>Philip</u> with this idle talke,

Which I remit, in hope this mood will die.   350

Bastard

    Nay Ladie mother, heare me further yet,

    For strong conceipt drives dutie hence awhile:

    Your husband <u>Fauconbridge</u> was Father to that sonne,

    That carries marks of Nature like the Sire,

    The sonne that blotteth you with wedlocks breach,   355

    And holds my right, as lineall in discent

    From him whose forme was figured in his face.

    Can Nature so dissemble in her frame,

    To make the one so like as like may be,

    And in the other print no character   360

    To chalenge any marke of true discent?

    My brothers minde is base, and too too dull,

    To mount where <u>Philip</u> lodgeth his affects,

    And his externall graces that you view

    (Though I report it) counterpoise not mine: 365

    His constitution plaine debilitie,

    Requires the chayre, and mine the seate of steele.

Nay, what is he, or what am I to him?

When any one that knoweth how to carpe,

Will scarcely judge us both one Countrey borne.   370

This Madame, this, hath drove me from myselfe:

And here by heavens eternall lampes I sweare,

As cursed <u>Nero</u> with his mother did,

So I with you, if you resolve me not.

Margaret

Let mothers teares quench out thy angers fire,   375

And urge no further what thou doost require.

Bastard

Let sonnes entreatie sway the mother now,

Or els she dies: Ile not infringe my vow.

Margaret

Unhappy taske: must I recount my shame,

Blab my misdeedes, or by concealing die?   380

Some power strike me speechlesse for a time,

Or take from him awhile his hearings use.

Why wish I so, unhappy as I am?

The fault is mine, and he the faultie frute,   IB4^V

I blush, I faint, oh would I might be mute.   385

Bastard

Mother be briefe, I long to know my name.

Margaret

And longing dye to shrowd thy Mothers shame.

Bastard

Come Madame come, you neede not be so loth,

The shame is shared equall twixt us both.

Ist not a slacknes in me worthie blame,   390

To be so olde, and cannot write my name.

Good Mother resolve me.

Margaret

Then Philip heare thy fortune and my griefe,

My honours losse by purchase of thy selfe,

My shame, thy name, and husbands secret wrong,   395

All maind and staind by youths unruly sway.

And when thou knowest from whence thou art extraught,

Or if thou knewst what sutes, what threates, what feares,

To moove by love, or massacre by death,

To yeeld with love, or end by loves contempt,   400
The mightines of him that courted me,
Who tempred terror with his wanton talke,
That something may extenuate the guilt.
But let it not advantage me so much:
Upbraid me rather with the Romane Dame   405
That shed her blood to wash away her shame.
Why stand I to expostulate the crime
With pro et contra, now the deede is don,
When to conclude two words may tell the tale,
That Philips Father was a Princes Son,   410
Rich Englands rule, worlds onely terror hee,
For honours losse left me with childe of thee:
Whose Sonne thou art, then pardon me the rather,
For faire King Richard was thy noble Father.

Bastard

Then Robin Fauconbridge I wish thee joy,   415
My Sire a King, and I a landles Boy.
Gods Ladie Mother, the world is in my debt,
There's something owing to Plantaginet.
I marrie Sir, let me alone for game,

Ile act some wonders now I know my name.   IC1   420
By blessed Marie Ile not sell that pride
For Englands wealth, and all the world beside.
Sit fast the proudest of my Fathers foes,
Away good Mother, there the comfort goes.   Exeunt.

Scene ii
Enter Philip the French King, and Lewes, Limoges,
Constance, and her sonne Arthur.

K. Philip

Now gin we broach the title of thy claime
Yong Arthur in the Albion Territories,
Scaring proud Angiers with a puissant siedge:
Brave Austria, cause of Cordelions death,
Is also come to aide thee in thy warres;   5
And all our Forces joyne for Arthurs right.
And, but for causes of great consequence,
Pleading delay till newes from England come,
Twice should not Titan hide him in the West,
To coole the fet-locks of his wearie teame,   10

Till I had with an unresisted shock

Controld the mannage of proud <u>Angiers</u> walls,

Or made a forfet of my fame to Chaunce.

Constance

May be that <u>John</u> in conscience or in feare

To offer wrong where you impugne the ill,   15

Will send such calme conditions backe to <u>Fraunce,</u>

As shall rebate the edge of fearefull warres:

If so, forbearance is a deede well done.

Arthur

Ah Mother, possession of a Crowne is much,

And <u>John</u> as I have heard reported of,   20

For present vantage would adventure farre.

The world can witnes in his Brothers time,

He tooke upon him rule and almost raigne:

Then must it follow as a doubtfull poynt,

That hee'le resigne the rule unto his Nephew.   25

I rather thinke the menace of the world

Sounds in his eares as threats of no esteeme,

And sooner would he scorne <u>Europaes</u> power,   IC1^v

Than loose the smallest title he enjoyes;

For questionles he is an Englishman.   30

Lewes

    Why are the English peereles in compare?

    Brave Cavaliers as ere that Iland bred,

    Have livde and dyde, and darde and done inough,

    Yet never gracde their Countrey for the cause:

    <u>England</u> is <u>England,</u> yeelding good and bad,   35

    And <u>John</u> of <u>England</u> is as other <u>Johns</u>.

    Trust me yong <u>Arthur,</u> if thou like my reede,

    Praise thou the French that helpe thee in this neede.

Lymoges

    The Englishman hath little cause I trow,

    To spend good speaches on so proud a foe.   40

    Why <u>Arthur</u> heres his spoyle that now is gon,

    Who when he livde outrovde his Brother <u>John:</u>

    But hastie curres that lie so long to catch,

    Come halting home, and meete their overmatch.

    But newes comes now, heres the Embassadour.   45

Enter Chattilion.

K. Philip

And in good time, welcome my Lord Chattilion:

What newes? will John accord to our commaund.

Chattilion

Be I not briefe to tell your Highnes all,

He will approach to interrupt my tale:

For one selfe bottome brought us both to Fraunce.   50

He on his part will try the chaunce of warre,

And if his words inferre assured truth,

Will loose himselfe and all his followers,

Ere yeeld unto the least of your demaunds.

The Mother Queene she taketh on amaine   55

Gainst Ladie Constance, counting her the cause

That doth effect this claime to Albion,

Conjuring Arthur with a Grandames care,

To leave his Mother; willing him submit

His state to John and her protection,   60

Who (as she saith) are studious for his good:

More circumstance the season intercepts:

This is the summe, which briefly I have showne.   IC2

K. Philip

This bitter winde must nip some bodies spring,

Sodaine and briefe, why so, tis harvest weather.   65

But say Chattilion, what persons of accompt are with him?

Chattilion

Of England Earle Pembrooke and Salsbury,

The onely noted men of any name.

Next them a Bastard of the Kings deceast,

A hardy wilde head, tough and venturous,   70

With many other men of high resolve.

Then is there with them Elinor Mother Queene,

And Blanch her Neece daughter to the King of Spaine:

These are the prime Birds of this hot adventure.

Enter John and his followers, Queene, Blanch, Bastard,

Earles of Pembrooke and Salisbury, etc.

K. Philip

Me seemeth John an over-daring spirit   75

Effects some frenzie in thy rash approach,

Treading my Confines with thy armed Troupes.

I rather lookt for some submisse reply

Touching the claime thy Nephew Arthur makes

To that which thou unjustly dost usurpe.   80

K. John

    For that <u>Chattilion</u> can discharge you all,

    I list not plead my Title with my tongue.

    Nor came I hether with intent of wrong

    To <u>Fraunce</u> or thee, or any right of thine;

    But in defence and purchase of my right,   85

    The Towne of <u>Angiers:</u> which thou doost begirt

    In the behalfe of Ladie <u>Constance</u> Sonne,

    Wheretoo nor he nor she can lay just claime.

<u>Constance</u>

    Yes (false intruder) if that just be just,

    And headstrong usurpation put apart,   90

    <u>Arthur</u> my Sonne, heire to thy elder Brother,

    Without ambiguous shadow of discent,

    Is Soueraigne to the substance thou withholdst.

<u>Elinor</u>

    Misgovernd Gossip, staine to this resort,

    Occasion of these undecided jarres,   95

    I say (that know) to check thy vaine suppose,

    Thy Sonne hath naught to doo with that he claymes.

For proofe whereof, I can inferre a Will,   IC2^V

That barres the way he urgeth by discent.

Constance

    A Will indeede, a crabbed Womans will,   100

    Wherein the Divell is an overseer,

    And proud dame Elnor sole Executresse:

    More wills than so, on perill of my soule,

    Were never made to hinder Arthurs right.

Arthur

    But say there was, as sure there can be none,   105

    The law intends such testaments as voyd,

    Where right discent can no way be impeacht.

Elinor

    Peace Arthur peace, thy mother makes thee wings

    To soare with perill after Icarus,

    And trust me yongling for thy Fathers sake,   110

    I pitie much the hazard of thy youth.

Constance

    Beshrew you els how pitifull you are,

    Readie to weepe to heare him aske his owne;

    Sorrow betide such Grandames and such griefe,

    That minister a poyson for pure love.   115

    But who so blinde, as cannot see this beame,

    That you forsooth would keepe your cousin downe,

    For feare his Mother should be usde too well?

I theres the griefe, confusion catch the braine,

That hammers shifts to stop a Princes raigne.   120

Elinor

    Impatient, frantike, common slanderer,

    Immodest Dame, unnurtred quarreller,

    I tell thee I, not envie to thy Son,

    But justice makes me speake as I have don.

K. Philip

    But heres no proof that showes your son a King.   125

K. John

    What wants, my sword shal more at large set down.

Lewes

    But that may breake before the truth be knowne.

Bastard

    Then this may hold till all his right be showne.

Lymoges

    Good words sir sauce, your betters are in place.

Bastard

    Not you sir doughtie with your Lions case.   130

Blanch

    Ah joy betide his soule, to whom that spoile belongd

    Ah Richard how thy glorie here is wrongd.

Lymoges

    Me thinkes that Richards pride, and Richards fall,

Should be a president t'affright you all.   IC3

Bastard

   --What words are these? how doo my sinews shake?   135

   My Fathers foe clad in my Fathers spoyle,

   A thousand furies kindle with revendge,

   This hart that choller keepes a consistorie,

   Searing my inwards with a brand of hate:

   How doth Alecto whisper in mine eares?   140

   Delay not Philip, kill the villaine straight,

   Disrobe him of the matchles moniment

   Thy Fathers triumph ore the Savages,--

   Base heardgroome, coward, peasant, worse than a

          threshing slave,

   What makst thou with the Trophei of a King?   145

   Shamst thou not coystrell, loathsome dunghill swad,

   To grace thy carkasse with an ornament

   Too precious for a Monarchs coverture?

   Scarce can I temper due obedience

   Unto the presence of my Soveraigne,   150

   From acting outrage on this trunke of hate:

But arme thee traytor, wronger of renowme,

For by his soule I sweare, my Fathers soule,

Twice will I not review the Mornings rise,

Till I have torne that Trophei from thy back,   155

And split thy heart, for wearing it so long.

Philip hath sworne, and if it be not done,

Let not the world repute me Richards Sonne.

Lymoges

Nay soft sir Bastard, harts are not split so soone,

Let them rejoyce that at the ende doo win: 160

And take this lesson at thy foemans hand,

Pawne not thy life, to get thy Fathers skin.

Blanch

Well may the world speake of his knightly valor,

That winnes this hide to weare a Ladies favour.

Bastard

Ill may I thrive, and nothing brooke with mee,   165

If shortly I present it not to thee.

K. Philip

Lordings forbeare, for time is comming fast,

That deedes may trie what words cannot determine,

And to the purpose for the cause you come.   IC3^V

Me seemes you set right in chaunce of warre,   170

Yeelding no other reasons for your claime,

But so and so, because it shall be so.

So wrong shalbe subornd by trust of strength:

A Tyrants practize to invest himselfe,

Where weake resistance giveth wrong the way.   175

To check the which, in holy lawfull Armes,

I in the right of Arthur Geffreys Sonne,

Am come before this Citie of Angiers,

To barre all other false supposed clayme,

From whence or howsoere the error springs.   180

And in his quarrell on my Princely word,

Ile fight it out unto the latest man.

K. John

Know King of Fraunce, I will not be commaunded

By any power or Prince in Christendome,

To yeeld an instance how I hold mine owne,   185

More than to answere, that mine owne is mine.

But wilt thou see me parley with the Towne,

And heare them offer me alleageance,

Fealtie and homage, as true liege men ought.

K. <u>Philip</u>

Summon them, I will not beleeve it till I see it, and 190

when I see it Ile soone change it.

<u>They summon the Towne, the Citizens appeare upon</u>

<u>the walls</u>.

K. <u>John</u>

You men of <u>Angiers,</u> and as I take it my loyall Subjects,

I have summoned you to the walls: to dispute on my right,

were to thinke you doubtfull therein, which I am perswaded

you are not. In few words, our Brothers Sonne,   195

backt with the King of <u>Fraunce,</u> have beleagred your Towne

upon a false pretended title to the same: in defence

whereof I your liege Lord have brought our power to fence

you from the Usurper, to free your intended servitude, and

utterly to supplant the foemen, to my right and   200

your rest. Say then, who keepe you the Towne for?

<u>Citizen</u>

For our lawfull King.

K. John   IC4

I was no lesse perswaded: then in Gods name open your

gates, and let me enter.

Citizen

And it please your Highnes we comptroll not your title,   205

neither will we rashly admit your entrance: if you bee

lawfull King, with all obedience we keepe it to your use,

if not King, our rashnes to be impeached for yeelding, with-

out more considerate triall: we answere not as men lawles,

but to the behoofe of him that prooves lawfull.   210

K. John

I shall not come in then?

Citizen

No my Lord, till we know more.

K. Philip

Then heare me speake in the behalfe of Arthur Sonne of

Geffrey elder Brother to John, his title manifest without

contradiction to the Crowne and Kingdome of England,   215

with Angiers and divers Townes on this side the sea: will

you acknowledge him your liege Lord, who speaketh in my

word to intertaine you with all favours as beseemeth a
King to his subjects, or a friend to his wel—willers:
or stand to the perill of your contempt, when his   220
title is prooved by the sword.

Citizen

We answere as before till you have prooved one right,
we acknowledge none right, he that tries himselfe our
Soveraigne, to him will we remaine firme subjects, and
for him, and in his right we hold our Towne as   225
desirous to know the truth as loath to subscribe before
we knowe. More than this we cannot say, and more than
this we dare not doo.

K. Philip

Then John I defie thee in the name and behalfe of Arthur
Plantaginet thy King and cousin, whose right and   230
patrimonie thou detainest, as I doubt not ere the day
ende in a set battell make thee confesse; whereunto with
a zeale to right I challenge thee.

K. John

I accept the challenge, and turne the defiance to
thy throate.   Exeunt.   235
Excursions. The Bastard chaseth Lymoges the Austrich
Duke, and maketh him leave the Lyons skinne.

Bastard   IC4^V

And art thou gone, misfortune haunt thy steps,

And chill colde fear assaile thy times of rest.

Morpheus leave here thy silent Eban cave,

Besiedge his thoughts with dismall fantasies,

And ghastly objects of pale threatning Mors.   240

Affright him every minute with stearne lookes,

Let shadowe temper terror in his thoughts,

And let the terror make the coward mad,

And in his madnes let him feare pursute,

And so in frenzie let the peasant die.   245

Here is the ransome that allayes his rage,

The first freehold that Richard left his sonne:

With which I shall surprize his living foes,

As Hectors statue did the fainting Greekes.   Exit.

Enter the Kings Herolds with Trumpets to the wals of

Angiers: they summon the Towne, the Citizens appeare

upon the walls.

English Herold

John by the grace of God King of England, Lord of   250

Ireland, Anjou, Toraine, etc. demaundeth once againe

of you his subjects of Angiers, if you will quietly

surrender up the Towne into his hands?

French Herold

Philip by the grace of God King of Fraunce, demaundeth

in the behalfe of Arthur Duke of Britaine, if you   255

will surrender up the Towne into his hands, to the use

of the said Arthur.

Citizens

Herrolds goe tell the two victorious Princes,

That we the poore Inhabitants of Angiers,

Require a parle of their Majesties.   260

Herolds

We goe.

Enter the Kings, Queene Elianor, Blaunch, Bastard,

Lymoges, Lewes, Chattilion, Pembrooke, Salisbury,

Constance, and Arthur Duke of Britaine.

K. John

Herold, what answere doo the Townsmen send?

<u>K</u>. <u>Philip</u>   IDl

    Will <u>Angiers</u> yeeld to <u>Philip</u> King of <u>Fraunce</u>?

<u>English</u> <u>Herold</u>

    The Townsmen on the wals accept your Grace.

<u>French</u> <u>Herold</u>

    And crave a parley of your Majestie.   265

<u>K</u>. <u>John</u>

    You Citizens of <u>Angiers</u>, have your eyes

    Beheld the slaughter that our English bowes

    Have made upon the coward frawdfull French?

    And have you wisely pondred therewithall

    Your gaine in yeelding to the English King?   270

<u>K</u>. <u>Philip</u>

    Their losse in yeelding to the English King.

    But <u>John</u>, they saw from out their highest Towers

    The Chevaliers of <u>Fraunce</u> and crossebow shot

    Make lanes of slaughtred bodies through thine hoast,

    And are resolvde to yeelde to <u>Arthurs</u> right.   275

<u>K</u>. <u>John</u>

    Why <u>Philip,</u> though thou bravest it fore the walls,

    Thy conscience knowes that <u>John</u> hath wonne the field.

<u>K</u>. <u>Philip</u>

    What ere my conscience knows, thy Armie feeles

    That <u>Philip</u> had the better of the day.

Bastard

Philip indeede hath got the Lyons case,   280
Which here he holds to Lymoges disgrace.
Base Duke to flye and leave such spoyles behinde:
But this thou knewst of force to make mee stay.
It farde with thee as with the marriner,
Spying the hugie Whale, whose monstrous bulke   285
Doth beare the waves like mountaines fore the winde,
That throwes out emptie vessells, so to stay
His furie, while the ship doth saile away.
Philip tis thine: and fore this Princely presence,
Madame I humbly lay it at your feete,   290
Being the first adventure I atchievd,
And first exployt your Grace did enjoyne:
Yet many more I long to be enjoynd.

Blanch

Philip I take it, and I thee commaund
To weare the same as earst thy Father did: 295
Therewith receive this favour at my hands,
T'incourage thee to follow Richards fame.

Arthur

Ye Citizens of Angiers, are ye mute?

Arthur or John, say which shall be your King?   ID1^v

Citizen

   We care not which, if once we knew the right,   300

   But till we know we will not yeeld our right.

Bastard

   Might Philip counsell two so mightie Kings,

   As are the Kings of England and of Fraunce,

   He would advise your Graces to unite

   And knit your forces gainst these Citizens,   305

   Pulling their battered walls about their eares.

   The Towne once wonne then strive about the claime,

   For they are minded to delude you both.

Citizen

   Kings, Princes, Lords and Knights assembled here,

   The Citizens of Angiers all by me   310

   Entreate your Majestie to heare them speake:

   And as you like the motion they shall make,

   So to account and follow their advice.

K. John, K. Philip

   Speake on, we give thee leave.

Citizen

    Then thus: whereas that yong and lustie knight   315
    Incites you on to knit your kingly strengths:
    The motion cannot choose but please the good,
    And such as love the quiet of the State.
    But how my Lords, how should your strengths be knit?
    Not to oppresse your subjects and your friends,   320
    And fill the world with brawles and mutinies:
    But unto peace your forces should be knit
    To live in Princely league and amitie:
    Doo this, the gates of Angiers shall give way
    And stand wide open to your harts content.   325
    To make this peace a lasting bond of love,
    Remains one onely honorable meanes,
    Which by your pardon I shall here display.
    Lewes the Dolphin and the heire of Fraunce,
    A man of noted valor through the world,   330
    Is yet unmaried: let him take to wife
    The beauteous daughter of the King of Spaine,
    Neece to K. John, the lovely Ladie Blanche,
    Begotten on his Sister Elianor.

With her in marriage will her unckle give   ID2   335
Castles and Towers as fitteth such a match.
The Kings thus joynd in league of perfect love,
They may so deale with Arthur Duke of Britaine,
Who is but yong, and yet unmeete to raigne,
As he shall stand contented everie way.   340
Thus have I boldly (for the common good)
Delivered what the Citie gave in charge.
And as upon conditions you agree,
So shall we stand content to yeeld the Towne.

Arthur

A proper peace, if such a motion hold;   345
These Kings beare armes for me, and for my right,
And they shall share my lands to make them friends.

Elinor

Sonne John,
Follow this motion, as thou lovest thy mother,
Make league with Philip, yeeld to any thing: 350
Lewes shall have my Neece, and then be sure
Arthur shall have small succour out of Fraunce.

K. John

    Brother of <u>Fraunce,</u> you heare the Citizens:

    Then tell me, how you meane to deale herein.

Constance

    Why <u>John,</u> what canst thou give unto thy Neece,   355

    That hast no foote of land, but <u>Arthurs</u> right?

Lewes

    Byr Ladie Citizens, I like your choyce,

    A lovely Damsell is the Ladie <u>Blanche,</u>

    Worthie the heire of <u>Europe</u> for her pheere.

Constance

    What Kings, why stand you gazing in a trance?   360

    Why how now Lords? accursed Citizens

    To fill and tickle their ambicious eares,

    With hope of gaine, that springs from <u>Arthurs</u> losse.

    Some dismall Plannet at thy birthday raignd,

    For now I see the fall of all thy hopes.   365

K. Philip

    Ladie, and Duke of <u>Britaine,</u> know you both,

    The King of <u>Fraunce</u> respects his honor more,

    Than to betray his friends and favourers.

    Princesse of <u>Spaine,</u> could you affect my Sonne,

    If we upon conditions could agree?   370

Bastard   ID2^v

    --Swounds Madam, take an English Gentleman:

    Slave as I was, I thought to have moovde the match.--

    Grandame you made me halfe a promise once,

    That Lady Blanch should bring me wealth inough,

    And make me heire of store of English land.   375

Elinor

    Peace Philip, I will looke thee out a wife,

    We must with pollicie compound this strife.

Bastard

    If Lewes get her, well, I say no more:

    But let the frolicke Frenchman take no scorne,

    If Philip front him with an English horne.   380

K. John

    Ladie,

    What answere make you to the King of France?

    Can you affect the Dolphin for your Lord?

Blanch

    I thanke the King that likes of me so well,

    To make me Bride unto so great a Prince: 385

    But give me leave my Lord to pause on this,

    Least being too too forward in the cause,

    It may be blemish to my modestie.

Elinor

    Sonne John, and worthie Philip K. of Fraunce,

    Doo you confer awhile about the Dower,   390

    And I will schoole my modest Neece so well,

    That she shall yeeld assoone as you have done.

Constance

    I, theres the wretch that broacheth all this ill,

    Why flye I not upon the Beldames face,

    And with my nayles pull foorth her hatefull eyes.   395

Arthur

    Sweete Mother cease these hastie madding fits:

    For my sake, let my Grandame have her will.

    O would she with her hands pull forth my heart,

    I could affoord it to appease these broyles.

    But mother let us wisely winke at all: 400

    Least farther harmes ensue our hastie speach.

K. Philip

    Brother of England, what dowrie wilt thou give

    Unto my Sonne in marriage with thy Neece?

K. John

    First Philip knowes her dowrie out of Spaine

    To be so great as may content a King: 405

    But more to mend and amplifie the same,

    I give in money thirtie thousand markes.

For land I leave it to thine owne demaund.   ID3

K. Philip

Then I demaund <u>Volquesson, Torain, Main,</u>

<u>Poiters</u> and <u>Anjou,</u> these five Provinces,   410

Which thou as King of <u>England</u> holdst in <u>Fraunce:</u>

Then shall our peace be soone concluded on.

Bastard

No lesse than five such Provinces at once?

K. John

Mother:

What shall I doo? my brother got these lands   415

With much effusion of our English bloud:

And shall I give it all away at once?

Elinor

<u>John</u> give it him, so shalt thou live in peace,

And keepe the residue sanz jeopardie.

K. John

<u>Philip</u> bring forth thy Sonne, here is my Neece,   420

And here in mariage I doo give with her

From me and my Successors English Kings,

<u>Volquesson, Poiters, Anjou, Torain, Main,</u>

And thirtie thousand markes of stipend coyne.

Now Citizens, how like you of this match?   425

Citizen

    We joy to see so sweete a peace begun.

Lewes

    Lewes with Blanch shall ever live content.

    But now King John, what say you to the Duke?

    Father, speake as you may in his behalfe.

K. Philip

    K. John, be good unto thy Nephew here,   430

    And give him somewhat that shall please thee best.

K. John

    Arthur, although thou troublest Englands peace:

    Yet here I give thee Brittaine for thine owne,

    Together with the Earledome of Richmont,

    And this rich Citie of Angiers withall.   435

Elinor

    And if thou seeke to please thine Unckle John,

    Shalt see my Sonne how I will make of thee.

K. John

    Now every thing is sorted to this end,

    Lets in and there prepare the mariage rytes,

    Which in S. Maries Chappell presently   440

    Shalbe performed ere this Presence part.   Exeunt.

          Manent Constance and Arthur.

Arthur

    Madam good cheere, these drouping languishments

Adde no redresse to salve our awkward haps.   ID3^V
If heavens have concluded these events,
To small availe is bitter pensivenes: 445
Seasons will change, and so our present griefe
May change with them, and all to our reliefe.

Constance

Ah boy, thy yeares I see are farre too greene
To looke into the bottome of these cares.
But I, who see the poyse that weigheth downe   450
Thy weale, my wish, and all the willing meanes
Wherewith thy fortune and thy fame should mount.
What joy, what ease, what rest can lodge in me,
With whom all hope and hap doth disagree?

Arthur

Yet Ladies teares, and cares, and solemne shows,   455
Rather than helpes, heape up more worke for woes.

Constance

If any Power will heare a widdowes plaint,
That from a wounded soule implores revenge;
Send fell contagion to infect this Clyme,

This cursed Countrey, where the traytors breath,   460
Whose perjurie as prowd Briareus,
Beleaguers all the Skie with misbeliefe.
He promist Arthur, and he sware it too,
To fence thy right, and check thy foemans pride:
But now black-spotted Perjure as he is,   465
He takes a truce with Elnors damned brat,
And marries Lewes to her lovely Neece,
Sharing thy fortune, and thy birth-dayes gift
Betweene these lovers: ill betide the match.
And as they shoulder thee from out thy owne,   470
And triumph in a widowes tearefull cares:
So heavens crosse them with a thriftles course.
Is all the bloud yspilt on either part,
Closing the cranies of the thirstie earth,
Growne to a lovegame and a Bridall feast?   475
And must thy birthright bid the wedding banes?
Poore helples boy, hopeles and helples too,
To whom misfortune seemes no yoke at all.

Thy stay, thy state, thy imminent mishaps   ID4
Woundeth thy mothers thoughts with feeling care,   480
Why lookst thou pale? the colour flyes thy face,
I trouble now the fountaine of thy youth,
And make it moodie with my doles discourse,
Goe in with me, reply not lovely boy,
We must obscure this mone with melodie,   485
Least worser wrack ensue our malecontent.   Exeunt.

Scene iii

Enter the King of England, the King of Fraunce, Arthur,
Bastard, Lewes, Lymoges, Constance, Blanche, Chattilion,
Pembrooke, Salisburie, and Elianor.

K. John

This is the day, the long desired day,
Wherein the Realmes of England and of Fraunce
Stand highly blessed in a lasting peace.
Thrice happie is the Bridegroome and the Bride,
From whose sweete Bridale such a concord springs,   5
To make of mortall foes immortall friends.

Constance

    Ungodly peace made by an others warre.

Bastard

    --Unhappie peace, that ties thee from revenge.

    Rouse thee Plantaginet, live not to see

    The butcher of the great Plantiginet.--   10

    Kings, Princes, and ye Peeres of either Realmes,

    Pardon my rashnes, and forgive the zeale

    That caries me in furie to a deede

    Of high desert, of honour, and of armes.

    A boone O Kings, a boone doth Philip beg   15

    Prostrate upon his knee: which knee shall cleave

    Unto the superficies of the earth,

    Till Fraunce and England graunt this glorious boone.

K. John

    Speake Philip, England graunts thee thy request.

K. Philip

    And Fraunce confirmes what ere is in his power.   20

Bastard

    Then Duke sit fast, I levell at thy head,

    Too base a ransome for my fathers life.

    Princes, I crave the Combat with the Duke

That braves it in dishonor of my Sire.   ID4^v

Your words are past nor can you now reverse   25

The Princely promise that revives my soule,

Whereat me thinks I see his sinnews shake:

This is the boon (dread Lords) which granted once

Or life or death are pleasant to my soule;

Since I shall live and die in <u>Richards</u> right.   30

<u>Lymoges</u>

Base Bastard, misbegotten of a King.

To interrupt these holy nuptiall rytes

With brawles and tumults to a Dukes disgrace:

Let it suffice, I scorne to joyne in fight,

With one so farre unequall to my selfe.   35

<u>Bastard</u>

A fine excuse, Kings if you wilbe Kings,

Then keepe your words, and let us combat it.

<u>K</u>. <u>John</u>

<u>Philip</u>, we cannot force the Duke to fight,

Being a subject unto neither Realme:

But tell me <u>Austria,</u> if an English Duke   40

Should dare thee thus, wouldst thou accept the challendge?

Lymoges

    Els let the world account the Austrich Duke

    The greatest coward living on the Earth.

K. John

    Then cheere thee Philip, John will keepe his word,

    Kneele down, in sight of Philip King of Fraunce   45

    And all these Princely Lords assembled here,

    I gird thee with the sword of Normandie,

    And of that land I doo invest thee Duke:

    So shalt thou be in living and in land

    Nothing inferiour unto Austria.   50

Lymoges

    K. John, I tell thee flatly to thy face

    Thou wrongst mine honour: and that thou maist see

    How much I scorne thy new made Duke and thee,

    I flatly say, I will not be compeld:

    And so farewell Sir Duke of Low degree,   55

    Ile finde a time to match you for this geere.   Exit.

K. John

    Stay Philip, let him goe the honors thine.

Bastard

    I cannot live unles his life be mine.

Elinor

    Thy forwardnes this day hath joyd my soule,

And made me thinke my <u>Richard</u> lives in thee.   IE1   60

K. <u>Philip</u>

Lordings lets in, and spend the wedding day

In maskes and triumphs, letting quarrells cease.

<u>Enter</u> Pandulph, <u>a</u> <u>Cardynall</u> <u>from</u> Rome.

Pandulph

Stay King of <u>France,</u> I charge thee joyn not hands

With him that stands accurst of God and men.

Know <u>John,</u> that I <u>Pandulph</u> Cardinall of <u>Millaine,</u> and   65

Legate from the Sea of <u>Rome,</u> demaund of thee in the name

of our holy Father the Pope <u>Innocent,</u> why thou dost (con-

trarie to the lawes of our holy mother the Church, and our

holye father the Pope) disturbe the quiet of the Church,

and disanull the election of <u>Stephen</u> <u>Langhton,</u> whom   70

his Holines hath elected Archbishop of <u>Canterburie:</u> this

in his Holines name I demaund of thee?

K. <u>John</u>

And what hast thou or the Pope thy maister to doo to

demaund of me, how I employ mine owne? Know sir Priest as

I honour the Church and holy Churchmen, so I scorne to 75

be subject to the greatest Prelate in the world. Tell thy

Maister so from me, and say, John of England said it, that
never an Italian Priest of them all, shall either have
tythe, tole, or poling penie out of England, but as I am
King, so wil I raigne next under God, supreame head   80
both over spirituall and temrall: and hee that contradicts
me in this, Ile make him hoppe headlesse.

K. Philip

What King John, know you what you say, thus to blaspheme
against our holy father the Pope.

K. John

Philip, though thou and all the Princes of Christendome 85
suffer themselves to be abusde by a Prelates slaverie, my
minde is not of such base temper. If the Pope will bee
King in England, let him winne it with the sword, I know
no other title he can alleage to mine inheritance.

Pandulph

John, this is thine answere?   90

K. John

What then?

Pandulph

Then I Pandulph of Padoa, Legate from the Apostolick Sea, doo in the name of S. Peter and his   1E1^v

successor our holy Father Pope Innocent, pronounce thee

accursed discharging every of thy subjectes of all   95

dutie and fealtie that they doo owe to thee, and pardon

and forgivenes of sinne to those or them whatsoever, which

shall carrie armes against thee, or murder thee: this I

pronounce, and charge all good men to abhorre thee as an

excommunicate person.   100

K. John

So sir, the more the Fox is curst the better a fares: if

God blesse me and my Land, let the Pope and his shavelings

curse and spare not.

Pandulph

Furthermore I charge thee Philip King of France, and al

the Kings and Princes of Christendome, to make war   105

uppon this miscreant: and whereas thou hast made a league

with him, and confirmed it by oath, I doo in the name of

our foresaid father the Pope, acquit thee of that oath as

unlawful, being made with an heretike, how saist thou

Philip, doost thou obey?   110

K. John

Brother of Fraunce, what say you to the Cardinall?

K. Philip

    I say, I am sorrie for your Majestie, requesting you to

    submit your selfe to the Church of Rome.

K. John

    And what say you to our league, if I doo not submit?

K. Philip

    What should I say? I must obey the Pope.   115

K. John

    Obey the Pope, and breake your oath to God?

K. Philip

    The Legate hath absolvde me of mine oath:

    Then yeeld to Rome, or I defie thee heere.

K. John

    Why Philip, I defie the Pope and thee,

    False as thou art, and perjurde K. of Fraunce,   120

    Unworthie man to be accompted King.

    Giv'st thou thy sword into a Prelates hands?

    Pandulph, where I of Abbots, Monkes and Friers

    Have taken somewhat to maintaine my warres,

    Now will I take no more but all they have.   125

    Ile rowze the lazie lubbers from their Cells,

    And in despight Ile send them to the Pope.

    Mother, come you with me, and for the rest

    That will not follow John in this attempt,

Confusion light upon their damned soules.   IE2   130

Come Lords,

Fight for your King that fighteth for your good.

>   Exeunt <u>King</u> John <u>and</u> <u>his</u> <u>followers.</u>

<u>K</u>. Philip

And are they gone? <u>Pandulph</u> thy selfe shalt see

How <u>Fraunce</u> will fight for <u>Rome</u> and <u>Romish</u> rytes.

Nobles, to armes, let him not passe the seas,   135

Lets take him captive, and in triumph lead

The K. of <u>England</u> to the gates of <u>Rome</u>.

<u>Arthur</u>, bestirre thee man, and thou shalt see

What <u>Philip</u> K. of <u>Fraunce</u> will do for thee.

<u>Blanch</u>

And will your Grace upon your wedding day   140

Forsake your Bride and follow dreadfull drums:

Nay, good my Lord, stay you at home with mee.

<u>Lewes</u>

Sweete heart content thee, and we shall agree.

<u>K</u>. Philip

Follow me Lords, Lord Cardynall lead the way,

Drums shalbe musique to this wedding day.   <u>Exeunt.</u>   145

Excursions. The Bastard pursues Austria, and kills him.

Bastard

Thus hath K. Richards Sonne performde his vowes.

And offred Austrias bloud for sacrifice

Unto his fathers everliving soule.

Brave Cordelion, now my heart doth say,

I have deservde, though not to be thy heire   150

Yet as I am, thy base begotten sonne,

A name as pleasing to thy Philips heart,

As to be cald the Duke of Normandie.

Lie there a pray to every ravening fowle:

And as my Father triumpht in thy spoyles,   155

And trode thine Ensignes underneath his feete,

So doo I tread upon thy cursed selfe,

And leave thy bodie to the fowles for food.

                         Exit with Lymoges body.

Excursions. Enter Arthur, Constance, Lewes, having taken

Q. Elianor prisoner.

Constance   IE2^V

Thus hath the God of Kings with conquering arme

Dispearst the foes to true succession.   165

Proud, and disturber of thy Countreyes peace,

Constance doth live to tame thine insolence,

And on thy head will now avenged be

For all the mischiefes hatched in thy braine.

Elinor

Contemptuous dame unreverent Dutches thou,   165

To brave so great a Queene as Elianor.

Base scolde hast thou forgot, that I was wife,

And mother to three mightie English Kings?

I charge thee then, and you forsooth sir Boy,

To set your Grandmother at libertie,   170

And yeeld to John your Unckle and your King.

Constance

Tis not thy words proud Queene shal carry it.

Elinor

Nor yet thy threates proud Dame shal daunt my minde.

Arthur

Sweete Grandame, and good Mother leave these brawles.

Elinor

    Ile finde a time to triumph in thy fall.   175

Constance

    My time is now to triumph in thy fall,

    And thou shalt know that Constance will triumph.

Arthur

    Good Mother weigh it is Queene Elianor,

    Though she be captive, use her like herselfe.

    Sweete Grandame beare with what my Mother sayes,   180

    Your Highnes shalbe used honourably.

                Enter a Messenger.

Messenger

    Lewes my Lord, Duke Arthur, and the rest,

    To armes in hast, K. John relyes his men,

    And ginnes the fight afresh: and sweares withall

    To lose his life, or set his Mother free.   185

Lewes

    Arthur away, tis time to looke about.

Elinor

    Why how now dame, what is your courage coold?

Constance

    No Elianor, my courage gathers strength,

And hopes to lead both <u>John</u> and thee as slaves: IE3

And in that hope, I hale thee to the field. <u>Exeunt</u>.   190

<u>Excursions</u>. Elianor <u>is</u> <u>rescued</u> <u>by</u> John, <u>and</u> Arthur <u>is</u>

<u>taken</u> <u>prisoner</u>. Exeunt. <u>Sound</u> <u>victorie</u>.

Scene iv

<u>Enter</u> John, Elinor, <u>and</u> Arthur <u>Prisoner</u>, <u>Bastard</u>,

Pembrooke, Salisbury, <u>and</u> Hubert de Burgh.

<u>K</u>. John

   Thus right triumphs, and <u>John</u> triumphs in right.

   <u>Arthur</u> thou seest, <u>Fraunce</u> cannot bolster thee:

   Thy Mothers pride hath brought thee to this fall.

   But if at last, Nephew thou yeeld thy selfe

   Into the gardance of thine Unckle <u>John</u>,   5

   Thou shalt be used as becomes a Prince.

<u>Arthur</u>

   Unckle, my Grandame taught her Nephew this,

   To **beare** captivitie with patience.

   Might hath prevayld not right, for I am King

   Of <u>England</u>, though thou weare the Diadem.   10

Elinor

 Sonne John, soone shall we teach him to forget

 These proud presumptions, and to know himselfe.

K. John

 Mother, he never will forget his claime,

 I would he livde not to remember it.

 But leaving this, we will to England now,   15

 And take some order with our Popelings there,

 That swell with pride, and fat of lay mens lands.

 Philip I make thee chiefe in this affaire,

 Ransack the Abbeys, Cloysters, Priories,

 Convert their coyne unto my souldiers use: 20

 And whatsoere he be within my Land,

 That goes to Rome for justice and for law,

 While he may have his right within the Realme,

 Let him be judgde a traitor to the State,

 And suffer as an enemie to England.   25

 Mother, we leave you here beyond the seas,

 As Regent of our Provinces in Fraunce,

While we to England take a speedie course,   IE3^V

And thanke our God that gave us victorie.

Hubert de Burgh take Arthur here to thee,   30

Be he thy prisoner: Hubert keepe him safe,

For on his life doth hang thy Soveraignes crowne,

But in his death consists thy Soveraignes blisse:

Then Hubert, as thou shortly hearst from me,

So use the prisoner I have given in charge.   35

Hubert

    Frolick yong Prince, though I your keeper bee,

    Yet shall your keeper live at your commaund.

Arthur

    As please my God, so shall become of me.

Elinor

    My Sonne to England, I will see thee shipt,

    And pray to God to send thee safe ashore.   40

Bastard

    Now warres are done, I long to be at home

    To dive into the Monkes and Abbots bags,

    To make some sport among the smooth skin Nunnes,

    And keepe some revell with the fauzen Friers.

K. John

    To England Lords, each looke unto your charge,   45

    And arme yourselves against the Romane pride.   Exeunt.

Scene v

Enter the K. of Fraunce, Lewes his sonne, and Cardinall
Pandolph Legate.

K. Philip

What every man attacht with this mishap?

Why frowne you so, why droop ye Lords of Fraunce?

Me thinkes it differs from a warlike minde

To lowre it for a checke or two of chaunce.

Had Lymoges escapt the bastards spight,   5

A little sorrow might have servde our losse.

Brave Austria, heaven joyes to have thee there.

Pandulph

His sowle is safe and free from Purgatorie,

Our holy Father hath dispenst his sinnes,

The blessed Saints have heard our orisons,   10

And all are Mediators for his soule,

And in the right of these most holy warres,

His holines free pardon doth pronounce

To all that follow you gainst English heretiques,   IE4

Who stand accursed in our mother Church.   15

Enter Constance alone.

K. Philip

To aggravate the measure of our griefe,

All malcontent comes Constance for her Sonne.

Be briefe good Madame, for your face imports

A tragick tale behinde thats yet untolde.

Her passions stop the organ of her voyce,   20

Deepe sorrow throbbeth misbefalne events,

Out with it Ladie, that our Act may end

A full Catastrophe of sad laments.

Constance

My tongue is tunde to storie forth mishap:

When did I breath to tell a pleasing tale?   25

Must Constance speake? let teares prevent her talke:

Must I discourse? let Dido sigh and say,

She weepes againe to heare the wrack of Troy:

Two words will serve, and then my tale is done:

Elnors proud brat hath robd me of my Sonne.   30

Lewes

Have patience Madame, this is chaunce of warre:

He may be ransomde, we revenge his wrong.

Constance

Be it ner so soone, I shall not live so long.

K. Philip

Despaire not yet, come Constance, goe with me,

These clowdes will fleet, the day will cleare againe.   35

Exeunt K. Philip and Constance.

Pandulph

Now Lewes, thy fortune buds with happie spring,

Our holy Fathers prayers effecteth this.

Arthur is safe, let John alone with him,

Thy title next is fairst to Englands Crowne:

Now stirre thy Father to begin with John,   40

The Pope sayes I, and so is Albion thine.

Lewes

Thankes my Lord Legate for your good conceipt,

Tis best we follow now the game is faire,

My Father wants to worke him your good words.

Pandulph

A few will serve to forward him in this,   45

Those shal not want: but lets about it then.   Exeunt.

Scene vi   IE4^V

Enter Philip and Attendants leading Thomas, a Frier,
charging him to show where the Abbots golde lay, Frier
Anthony following.

Bastard

Come on you fat Franciscans, dallie no longer, but shew me
where the Abbots treasure lyes, or die.

Frier Thomas

Benedicamus Domini,

Was ever such an injurie.

Sweete S. Withold of thy lenitie,   5

Defend us from extremitie,

And heare us for S. Charitie,

Oppressed with austeritie.

In nomini Domini,

Make I my homilie,   10

Gentle Gentilitie

Grieve not the Cleargie.

Bastard

Grey gownd good face, conjure ye, ner trust me
            for a groate,

If this waste girdle hang thee not that girdeth in
            thy coate.

Now balde and barefoote Bungie birds when up the   15
            gallowes climing,

Say <u>Philip</u> he had words inough to put you downe
  with ryming.

<u>Frier Thomas</u>

 A pardon, <u>O parce,</u>

 Saint <u>Fraunces</u> for mercie,

 Shall shield thee from nightspells

 And dreaming of divells,   20

 If thou wilt forgive me,

 And never more grieve me,

 With fasting and praying,

 And <u>Haile</u> <u>Marie</u> saying,

 From black Purgatorie   25

 A penance right sorie,

 Frier <u>Thomas</u> will warme you,

 It shall never harme you.

<u>Bastard</u>

 Come leave off your rabble,

 Sirs hang up this lozell.   30

<u>Frier Anthony</u>

 For charitie I beg his life, Saint <u>Frauncis</u> chiefest
   Frier,

 The best in all our Covent Sir, to keepe a Winters fier.

 O strangle not the good olde man, my hostesse oldest
   guest,

 And I will bring you by and by unto the Priors chest.

Bastard   IF1

    I, saist thou so, and if thou wilt the frier is   35

        at libertie,

    If not, as I am honest man, Ile hang you both for companie.

Frier Anthony

    Come hether, this is the chest though simple to behold

    That wanteth not a thousand pound in silver and in gold.

    My selfe will warrant full so much, I know the Abbots

        store,

    Ile pawne my life there is no lesse to have what ere   40

        is more.

Bastard

    I take thy word, the overplus unto thy share shall come,

    But if there want of full so much, thy neck shall pay

        the sum.

    Breake up the Cofer, Frier.

Frier Anthony

    Oh I am undun,

    Faire Alice the Nun   45

    Hath tooke up her rest

    In the Abbots chest,

    Sancte benedicite,

    Pardon my simplicitie.

    Fie Alice, confession   50

    Will not salve this transgression.

Bastard

    What have wee here, a holy Nun? So keep mee God in health,

A smooth facte Nunne (for ought I knowe) is all the
      Abbots wealth.
Is this the Nonries chastitie?   Beshrewe me but I thinke
They goe as oft to Venery, as niggards to their drinke. 55
Why paltrey Frier and Pandar too, yee shamelesse shaven
      crowne,
Is this the chest that held a hoord, at least a thousand
      pound?
And is the hoord a holy whore?   Wel be the hangman nimble,
Hee'le take the paine to paye you home, and teach you
      to dissemble.

Nunne Alice

O spare the Frier Anthony, a better never was   60
To sing a Dirige solemnly, or read a morning Masse.
If money be the meanes of this, I know an ancient Nunne,
That hath a hoord this seaven yeares, did never see
      the sunne;
And that is yours, and what is ours, so favour now be shown,
You shall commaund as commonly, as if it were your owne. 65

Frier Thomas

Your honour excepted.

Nunne Alice

         I Thomas, I meane so.

Bastard

From all save from Friers.

Nunne Alice

         Good Sir, doo not thinke so?

Bastard   IF1^v

I thinke and see so: why how camst thou here?

Frier Thomas

To hide her from lay men.

Nunne Alice

Tis true sir, for feare.

Bastard

For feare of the laytie: a pitifull dred   70

When a Nunne flies for succour to a fat Friers bed.

But now for your ransome my Cloyster-bred Conney,

To the chest that you speake of where lyes so much money.

Nunne Alice

Faire Sir, within this presse, of plate and money is

The valew of a thousand markes, and other thing by gis.   75

Let us alone, and take it all, tis yours Sir, now you know it.

Bastard

Come on sir Frier, pick the locke, this geere dooth cotton

hansome,

That covetousnes so cunningly must pay the letchers ransom.

What is in the hoord?

Frier Thomas

Frier Laurence my Lord, now holy water help us,   80

Some witch, or some divell is sent to delude us:

Haud credo Laurentius,

That thou shouldst be pend thus

In the presse of a Nun.

We are all undon,   85

And brought to discredence

If thou be Frier <u>Laurence</u>.

<u>Frier</u> <u>Laurence</u>

<u>Amor</u> <u>vincit</u> <u>omnia,</u> so <u>Cato</u> affirmeth,

And therefore a Frier whose fancie soone burneth:

Because he is mortall and made of mould,   90

He omits what he ought, and doth more than he should.

Bastard

How goes this geere? the Friers chest filde with a fausen

       Nunne,

The Nunne again locks Frier up, to keep him from the Sun.

Belike the presse is purgatorie, or penance passing

       grievous:

The Friers chest a hel for Nuns. How do these dolts   95

       deceive us?

Is this the labour of their lives to feede and live

       at ease,

To revell so lasciviously as often as they please.

Ile mend the fault or fault my ayme, if I do misse

       amending,

Tis better burn the cloisters down than leave them for

       offending.

But holy you, to you I speake, to you religious divell,100

Is this the presse that holdes the summe to quite you

       for your evill.

<u>Nunne</u> <u>Alice</u>

I crie <u>Peccavi,</u> <u>parce</u> <u>me,</u> good Sir I was beguild.

Frier Thomas   IF2

Absolve Sir for charitie she would be reconcilde.

Bastard

And so I shall, sirs binde them fast, this is their absolution,

Go hang them up for hurting them, hast them to execution. 105

Frier Laurence

O tempus edax rerum,

Geve children bookes they teare them.

O vanitas vanitatis,

In this waning aetatis,

At threescore welneere   110

To goe to this geere,

To my conscience a clog

To dye like a dog.

Exaudi me Domine,

Si vis me parce   115

Dabo pecuniam,

Si habeo veniam

To goe and fetch it,

I will dispatch it,

A hundred pound sterling   120

For my lives sparing.

                Enter Peter a Prophet, with people.

Peter

Hoe, who is here, S. Fraunces be your speed,

Come in my flock, and follow me, your fortunes I will reed

Come hether boy, goe get thee home, and clime not overhie:

For from aloft thy fortunes stands in hazard thou shalt die. 125

Boy

    God be with you Peter, I pray

    You come to our house a Sunday.

Peter

    My boy show me thy hand, blesse thee

    My boy, for in thy palme I see

    A many troubles are ybent to dwell,   130

    But thou shalt scape them all and doo full well.

Boy

    I thanke you Peter, theres a cheese for your labor: my

    sister prayes ye to come home, and tell her how many hus-

    bands she shall have, and shee'l give you a rib of bacon.

Peter

    My masters, stay at the towns end for me, Ile come to 135

    you all anon: I must dispatch some busines with a Frier,

    and then Ile read your fortunes.

Bastard

    How now, a Prophet? Sir prophet whence are ye?

Peter

    I am of the world and in the world, but live not as others

    by the world: what I am I know, and what thou wilt   140

    be I know. If thou knowest me now be answered: if not,

    enquire no more what I am.

Bastard

    Sir, I know you will be a dissembling knave, that deludes

    the people with blinde prophecies: you are him I looke

for, you shall away with me: bring away all the rabble, 145
and you Frier <u>Laurence</u> remember your raunsome   IF2^V
a hundred pound, and a pardon for your selfe, and the
rest.   Come on Sir Prophet, you shall with me, to receive
a Prophets rewarde.   <u>Exeunt.</u>

Scene **vii**

              <u>Enter</u> Hubert de Burgh <u>with</u> <u>three</u> <u>men.</u>

<u>Hubert</u>

My masters, I have shewed you what warrant I have for this
attempt; I perceive by your heavie countenances, you had
rather be otherwise imployed, and for my owne part, I
would the King had made choyce of some other executioner:
onely this is my comfort, that a King commaunds, whose   5
precepts neglected or omitted, threatneth torture for the
default.   Therefore in briefe, leave me, and be readie to
attend the adventure: stay within that entry, and when you
heare me crie, <u>God</u> <u>save</u> <u>the</u> <u>King,</u> issue sodainly foorth,
lay handes on <u>Arthur,</u> set him in this chayre, wherin   10
(once fast bound) leave him with mee to finish the rest.

Attendants

    We goe, though loath.   Exeunt.

Hubert

    My Lord, will it please your Honour to take the benefite

    of the faire evening?

                Enter Arthur to Hubert de Burgh.

Arthur

    Gramercie Hubert for thy care of me,   15

    In one to whom restraint is newly knowen,

    The joy of walking is small benefit,

    Yet will I take thy offer with small thankes,

    I would not loose the pleasure of the eye.

    But tell me curteous keeper if you can,   20

    How long the King will have me tarrie heere.

Hubert

    I know not Prince, but as I gesse not long.

    God send you freedome, and God save the King.

                 They issue forth.

Arthur

    Why how now sirs, what may this outrage meane?

O helpe me <u>Hubert,</u> gentle keeper helpe: IF3   25

God **send** this sodaine mutinous approach

Tend not to reave a wretched guiltles life.

Hubert

So sirs, depart, and leave the rest for me.

<u>Exeunt</u> <u>Attendants</u>.

Arthur

Then <u>Arthur</u> yeeld, death frowneth in thy face,

What meaneth this? Good <u>Hubert</u> plead the case.   30

Hubert

Patience yong Lord, and listen words of woe,

Harmfull and harsh, hells horror to be heard:

A dismall tale fit for a furies tongue.

I faint to tell, deepe sorrow is the sound.

Arthur

What, must I die?   35

Hubert

No newes of death, but tidings of more hate,

A wrathfull doome, and most unluckie fate:

Deaths dish were daintie at so fell a feast,

Be deafe, heare not, its hell to tell the rest.

Arthur

    Alas thou wrongst my youth with words of feare,   40

    Tis hell, tis horror, not for one to heare:

    What is it man if it must needes be don,

    Act it, and end it, that the paine were gon.

Hubert

    I will not chaunt such dolour with my tongue,

    Yet must I act the outrage with my hand.   45

    My heart my head, and all my powers beside,

    To aide the office have at once denide.

    Peruse this letter, lines of treble woe,

    Read ore my charge, and pardon when you know.

Arthur

    Hubert these are to commaund thee, as thou tendrest   50

    our quiet in minde and the estate of our person, that

    presently upon the receipt of our commaund, thou put out

    the eyes of Arthur Plantaginet.

    Ah monstrous damned man,

    His very breath infects the elements,   55

    Contagious venyme dwelleth in his heart,

    Effecting meanes to poyson all the world.

    Unreverent may I be to blame the heavens

Of great injustice, that the miscreant   IF3^V

Lives to oppresse the innocents with wrong.   60

Ah Hubert, makes he thee his instrument

To sound the tromp that causeth hell triumph?

Heaven weepes, the Saints doo shed celestiall teares,

They feare thy fall, and cyte thee with remorse,

They knock thy conscience, mooving pitie there,   65

Willing to fence thee from the rage of hell:

Hell Hubert, trust me all the plagues of hell

Hangs on performance of this damned deede.

This seale, the warrant of the bodies blisse,

Ensureth Satan chieftaine of thy soule: 70

Subscribe not Hubert, give not Gods part away.

I speake not onely for eyes priviledge,

The chiefe exterior that I would enjoy:

But for thy perill, farre beyond my paine,

Thy sweete soules losse, more than my eyes vaine lack; 75

A cause internall, and eternall too.

Advise thee Hubert, for the case is hard,

To loose salvation for a Kings reward.

Hubert

My Lord, a subject dwelling in the land

Is tyed to execute the Kings commaund.   80

Arthur

    Yet God commands, whose power reacheth further,

    That no commaund should stand in force to murther.

Hubert

    But that same Essence hath ordaind a law,

    A death for guilt, to keepe the world in awe.

Arthur

    I plead not guiltie, treasonles and free.   85

Hubert

    But that appeale my Lord concernes not me.

Arthur

    Why, thou art he that maist omit the perill.

Hubert

    I, if my Soveraigne would remit his quarrell.

Arthur

    His quarrell is unhallowed false and wrong.

Hubert

    Then be the blame to whom it doth belong.   90

Arthur

    Why thats to thee if thou as they proceede,

    Conclude their judgement with so vile a deede.

Hubert

    Why then no execution can be lawfull,

    If Judges doomes must be reputed doubtfull.

Arthur   IF4

   Yes where in forme of Lawe in place and time,   95
   The offender is convicted of the crime.

Hubert

   My Lord, my Lord, this long expostulation,
   Heapes up more griefe, than promise of redresse;
   For this I know, and so resolvde I end,
   That subjects lives on Kings commaunds depend.   100
   I must not reason why he is your foe,
   But doo his charge since he commaunds it so.

Arthur

   Then doo thy charge, and charged be thy soule
   With wrongfull persecution done this day.
   You rowling eyes, whose superficies yet   105
   I doo behold with eyes that Nature lent:
   Send foorth the terror of your Moovers frowne,
   To wreake my wrong upon the murtherers
   That rob me of your faire reflecting view:
   Let hell to them (as earth they wish to mee)   110
   Be darke and direfull guerdon for their guylt,

And let the black tormenters of deepe <u>Tartary</u>
Upbraide them with this damned enterprise,
Inflicting change of tortures on their soules.
Delay not <u>Hubert,</u> my orisons are ended,   115
Begin I pray thee, reave me of my sight:
But to performe a tragedie indeede,
Conclude the period with a mortall stab.
<u>Constance</u> farewell, tormentor come away,
Make my dispatch the Tirants feasting day.   120

<u>Hubert</u>

I faint, I feare, my conscience bids desist:
Faint did I say, feare was it that I named?
My King commaunds, that warrant sets me free:
But God forbids, and he commaundeth Kings,
That great Commaunder counterchecks my charge,   125
He stayes my hand, he maketh soft my heart,
Goe cursed tooles, your office is exempt,
Cheere thee yong Lord, thou shalt not loose an eye,
Though I should purchase it with losse of life.
Ile to the King, and say his will is done,   130

And of the langor tell him thou art dead,   IF4^V

Goe in with me, for <u>Hubert</u> was not borne

To blinde those lampes that Nature pollisht so.

<u>Arthur</u>

<u>Hubert,</u> if ever <u>Arthur</u> be in state,

Looke for amends of this received gift   135

I tooke my eysight by thy curtesie,

Thou lentst them me, I will not be ingrate.

But now procrastination may offend

The issue that thy kindnes undertakes:

Depart we <u>Hubert</u> to prevent the worst.   <u>Exeunt.</u>   140

Scene viii

      <u>Enter</u> <u>King</u> John, Essex, Penbrooke.

<u>K</u>. <u>John</u>

Now warlike followers resteth ought undon

That may impeach us of fond oversight?

The French have felt the temper of our swords,

Cold terror keepes possession in their sowles,

Checking their overdaring arrogance   5

For buckling with so great an overmatch.

The Arche proud titled Priest of <u>Italy,</u>

That calles himselfe grand Viccar under God

Is busied now with trentall obsequies,

Masse and months minde, dirge and I know not what   10

To ease their sowles in painefull purgatory,

That have miscaried in these bloudy warres.

Heard you not Lords when first his holines

Had tidings of our small account of him,

How with a taunt vaunting upon his toes   15

He urgde a reason why the English Asse

Disdaignd the blessed ordinance of <u>Rome?</u>

The title (reverently might I inferre)

Became the Kings that earst have borne the load,

The slavish weight of that controlling Priest: 20

Who at his pleasure temperd them like waxe

To carrie armes on danger of his curse,

Banding their sowles with warrants of his hand.

I grieve to thinke how Kings in ages past

(Simply devoted to the Sea of <u>Rome</u>)   IG1   25

Have run into a thousand acts of shame.

But now for confirmation of our State,

Sith we have proynd the more than needfull braunch

That did oppresse the true wel-growing stock,

It resteth we throughout our Territories   30

Be reproclaimed and invested King.

<u>Pembrooke</u>

My Liege, that were to busie men with doubts,

Once were you crownd, proclaimd, and with applause

Your Citie streetes have ecchoed to the eare,

God save the King, God save our Soveraigne <u>John</u>.   35

Pardon my feare, my censure doth infer

Your Highnes not deposde from Regall State,

Would breed a mutinie in peoples mindes,

What it should meane to have you crownd againe.

<u>K</u>. <u>John</u>

<u>Pembrooke</u> performe what I have bid thee doo,   40

Thou knowst not what induceth me to this,

<u>Essex</u> goe in, and Lordings all be gon

About this taske, I will be crownd anon.   <u>Exeunt Lords</u>.

<u>Enter the Bastard.</u>

<u>Philip,</u> what newes, how doo the Abbots chests?

Are Friers fatter than the Nunnes are faire?   45

What cheere with Churchmen, had they golde or no?

Tell me how hath thy office tooke effect?

Bastard

My Lord, I have performd your Highnes charge:

The ease bred Abbots and the bare foote Friers,

The Monkes the Priors and holy cloystred Nunnes,   50

Are all in health, and were my Lord in wealth,

Till I had tythde and tolde their holy hoords.

I doubt not when your Highnes sees my prize,

You may proportion all their former pride.

<u>K. John</u>

Why so, now sorts it <u>Philip</u> as it should: 55

This small intrusion into Abbey trunkes,

Will make the Popelings excommunicate,

Curse, ban, and breath out damned orisons,   IG1^v

As thick as hailestones fore the springs approach:

But yet as harmles and without effect,   60

As is the eccho of a Cannons crack

Dischargd against the battlements of heaven.

But what newes els befell there <u>Philip?</u>

<u>Bastard</u>

Strange newes my Lord: within your territories,

Nere <u>Pomfret</u> is a Prophet new sprong up,   65

Whose divination volleys wonders foorth;

To him the Commons throng with Countrey gifts,

He sets a date unto the Beldames death,

Prescribes how long the Virgins state shall last,

Distinguisheth the mooving of the heavens,   70

Gives limits unto holy nuptiall rytes,

Foretelleth famine, aboundeth plentie forth,

Of fate, of fortune, life and death he chats,

With such assurance, scruples put apart,

As if he knew the certaine doomes of heaven,   75

Or kept a Register of all the Destinies.

K. John

    Thou telst me mervailes, would thou hadst brought the man,

    We might have questiond him of things to come.

Bastard

    My Lord, I tooke a care of had I wist,

    And brought the Prophet with me to the Court,   80

    He stayes my Lord but at the Presence doore:

    Pleaseth your Highnes, I will call him in.

K. John

    Nay stay awhile, wee'l have him here anon,

    A thing of weight is first to be performd.

    Enter the Nobles and Bishops and crowne King John, and

    then crie God save the King.

    Lordings and friends supporters of our state,   85

    Admire not at this unaccustomd course,

    Nor in your thoughts blame not this deede of yours.

    Once ere this time was I invested King,

    Your fealtie sworne as Liegmen to our state:

Once since that time ambicious weedes have sprung   IG2   90
To staine the beautie of our garden plot:
But heavens in our conduct rooting thence
The false intruders, breakers of worlds peace,
Have to our joy, made Sunshine chase the storme.
After the which, to try your constancie,   95
That now I see is worthie of your names,
We cravde once more your helps for to invest us
Into the right that envie sought to wrack.
Once was I not deposde, your former choyce;
Now twice been crowned and applauded King: 100
Your cheered action to install me so,
Infers assured witnes of your loves,
And binds me over in a Kingly care
To render love with love, rewards of worth
To ballance downe requitall to the full.   105
But thankes the while, thankes Lordings to you all:
Aske me and use me, try me and finde me yours.

Essex

A boon my Lord, at vauntage of your words
We aske to guerdon all our loyalties.

Pembrooke

We take the time your Highnes bids us aske: 110
Please it you graunt, you make your promise good,
With lesser losse than one superfluous haire
That not remembred falleth from your head.

K. John

My word is past, receive your boone my Lords.
What may it be? Aske it, and it is yours.   115

Essex

We crave my Lord, to please the Commons with
The libertie of Ladie Constance Sonne:
Whose durance darkeneth your Highnes right,
As if you kept him prisoner, to the end
Your selfe were doubtfull of the thing you have.   120
Dismisse him thence, your Highnes needes not feare,
Twice by consent you are proclaimd our King.

Pembrooke

This if you graunt, were all unto your good:
For simple people muse you keepe him close.

K. John

Your words have searcht the center of my thoughts,   125

Confirming warrant of your loyalties,   IG2^{v}

Dismisse your counsell, sway my state,

Let <u>John</u> doo nothing but by your consents.--

Why how now <u>Philip</u>, what extasie is this?

Why casts thou up thy eyes to heaven so?   130

<u>There</u> <u>the</u> <u>five</u> <u>Moones</u> <u>appeare.</u>

<u>Bastard</u>

See, see my Lord strange apparitions.

Glauncing mine eye to see the Diadem

Placte by the Bishops on your Highnes head,

From foorth a gloomie cloude, which curtaine like

Displaide it selfe, I sodainly espied   135

Five Moones reflecting, as you see them now:

Even in the moment that the Crowne was placte

Gan they appeare, holding the course you see.

<u>K</u>. <u>John</u>

What might portend these apparitions,

Unusuall signes, forerunners of event,   140

Presagers of strange terror to the world:

Beleeve me Lords the object feares me much.

<u>Philip</u> thou toldst me of a Wizzard late,

Fetch in the man to descant of this show.   <u>Exit</u> <u>Bastard.</u>

Pembrooke

The heavens frowne upon the sinfull earth,   145

When with prodigious unaccustomd signes

They spot their superficies with such wonder.

Essex

Before the ruin of <u>Jerusalem,</u>

Such Meteors were the Ensignes of his wrath

That hastned to destroy the faultfull Towne.   150

                <u>Enter</u> <u>the</u> <u>Bastard</u> <u>with</u> <u>the</u> <u>Prophet.</u>

<u>K</u>. <u>John</u>

Is this the man?

Bastard

It is my Lord.

<u>K</u>. <u>John</u>

Prophet of <u>Pomfret,</u> for so I heare thou art,

That calculatst of many things to come:

Who by a power repleate with heavenly gift   155

Canst blab the counsell of thy Makers will.   IG3
If fame be true, or truth be wrongd by thee,
Decide, in cyphering what these five Moones
Portend this Clyme, if they presage at all.
Breath out thy gift, and if I live to see   160
Thy divination take a true effect,
Ile honour thee above all earthly men.

Peter

The Skie wherein these Moones have residence,
Presenteth Rome the great Metropolis,
Where sits the Pope in all his holy pompe.   165
Fowre of the Moones present fowre Provinces,
To wit, Spaine, Denmarke, Germanie, and Fraunce,
That beare the yoke of proud commaunding Rome,
And stand in feare to tempt the Prelates curse.
The smallest Moone that whirles about the rest,   170
Impatient of the place he holds with them,
Doth figure foorth this Iland Albion,
Who gins to scorne the Sea and State of Rome,
And seekes to shun the Edicts of the Pope:

This showes the heaven, and this I doo averre   175
Is figured in these apparitions.

K. John

Why then it seemes the heavens smile on us,
Giving applause for leaving of the Pope.
But for they chaunce in our Meridian,
Doo they effect no private growing ill   180
To be inflicted on us in this Clyme?

Peter

The Moones effect no more than what I said:
But on some other knowledge that I have
By my prescience, ere Ascension day
Have brought the Sunne unto his usuall height,   185
Of Crowne, Estate, and Royall dignitie,
Thou shalt be cleane dispoyld and dispossest.

K. John

False Dreamer, perish with thy witched newes,
Villaine thou woundst me with thy fallacies:
If it be true, dye for thy tidings price;   190
If false, for fearing me with vaine suppose:

Hence with the Witch, hells damned secretarie.   IG3^V

Lock him up sure: for by my faith I sweare,

True or not true, the Wizzard shall not live.

                    <u>Exeunt</u> the <u>Bastard</u> <u>and</u> the <u>Prophet.</u>

--Before Ascension day: who should be cause hereof?   195

Cut off the cause and then the effect will dye.

Tut, tut, my mercie serves to maime my selfe,

The roote doth live, from whence these thornes spring up,

I and my promise past for his delivry:

Frowne friends, faile faith, the divell goe withall,   200

The brat shall dye, that terrifies me thus.--

<u>Pembrooke</u> and <u>Essex</u> I recall my graunt,

I will not buy your favours with my feare:

Nay murmur not, my will is law enough,

I love you well, but if I lovde you better,   205

I would not buy it with my discontent.

                       <u>Enter</u> Hubert.

How now, what newes with thee.

<u>Hubert</u>

     According to your Highnes strickt commaund

     Yong <u>Arthurs</u> eyes are blinded and extinct.

<u>K</u>. <u>John</u>

     Why so,   210

     Then he may feele the crowne, but never see it.

Hubert

Nor see nor feele, for of the extreame paine,

Within one hower gave he up the Ghost.

K. John

What is he dead?

Hubert

He is my Lord.   215

K. John

Then with him dye my cares.

Essex

Now joy betide thy soule.

Pembrooke

And heavens revenge thy death.

Essex

What have you done my Lord? Was ever heard

A deede of more inhumane consequence?   220

Your foes will curse, your friends will crie revenge.

Unkindly rage more rough than Northern winde,

To clip the beautie of so sweete a flower.

What hope in us for mercie on a fault,

When kinsman dyes without impeach of cause,   225

As you have done, so come to cheere you with,

The guilt shall never be cast me in my teeth.

                                        Exeunt Nobles.

K. <u>John</u>   IG4

--And are you gone?   The divell be your guide:

Proud Rebels as you are to brave me so:

Saucie, uncivill, checkers of my will.   230

Your tongues give edge unto the fatall knife:

That shall have passage through your traitrous throats.

But husht, breath not buggs words to soone abroad,

Least time prevent the issue of thy reach.

<u>Arthur</u> is dead, I there the corzie growes: 235

But while he livde, the danger was the more;

His death hath freed me from a thousand feares,

But it hath purchast me ten times ten thousand foes.

Why all is one, such luck shall haunt his game,

To whome the divell owes an open shame: 240

His life a foe that leveld at my crowne,

His death a frame to pull my building downe.

My thoughts harpt still on quiet by his end,

Who living aymed shrowdly at my roome:

But to prevent that plea twice was I crownd,   245

Twice did my subjects sweare me fealtie,

And in my conscience lovde me as their liege,

In whose defence they would have pawnd their lives.

But now they shun me as a Serpents sting,

A tragick Tyrant sterne and pitiles,   250

And not a title followes after John,

But Butcher, bloudsucker and murtherer,

What Planet governde my nativitie,

To bode me soveraigne types of high estate,

So interlacte with hellish discontent,   255

Wherein fell furie hath no interest.

Curst be the Crowne chiefe author of my care,

Nay curst my will that made the Crowne my care:

Curst be my birthday, curst ten times the wombe

That yeelded me alive into the world.--   260

Art thou there villaine, Furies haunt thee still,

For killing him whom all the world laments.

Hubert   IG4^V

Why heres my Lord your Highnes hand and seale,

Charging on lives regard to doo the deede.

K. John

Ah dull conceipted peazant knowst thou not,   265

It was a damned execrable deede:

Showst me a seale? Oh villaine, both our soules

Have solde their freedome to the thrall of hell,

Under the warrant of that cursed seale.

Hence villaine, hang thy selfe, and say in hell   270

That I am comming for a kingdome there.

Hubert

My Lord attend the happie tale I tell,

For heavens health send Sathan packing hence

That instigates your Highnes to despaire.

If Arthurs death be dismall to be heard,   275

Bandie the newes for rumors of untruth:

He lives my Lord the sweetest youth alive,

In health, with eysight, not a haire amisse.

This hart tooke vigor from this forward hand,

Making it weake to execute your charge.   280

K. John

What lives he?   Then sweete hope come home agen.

Chase hence despaire, the purveyer for hell.

Hye Hubert, tell these tidings to my Lords

That throb in passions for yong Arthurs death:

Hence Hubert, stay not till thou hast reveald   285

The wished newes of Arthurs happy health.

I goe my selfe, the joyfulst man alive

To storie out this new supposed crime.   Exeunt.

The ende of the first part.

THE   IIA1

Second part of the

troublesome Raigne of King

John, conteining the death

of Arthur Plantaginet,

the landing of Lewes, and

the poysning of King

John at Swinstead

Abbey.

As it was (sundry times) publikely acted by the

Queenes Majesties Players, in the ho-

nourable Citie of

London.

[ornament]

Imprinted at London for Sampson Clarke,

and are to be solde at his shop, on the backe-

side of the Royall Exchange.

1591.

To the Gentlmen Readers.   IIA2

The changeles purpose of determinde Fate
Gives period to our care, or harts content,
When heavens fixt time for this or that hath end:
Nor can earths pomp or pollicie prevent
The doome ordained in their secret will.   5
  Gentles we left King <u>John</u> repleate with blisse
That <u>Arthur</u> livde, whom he supposed slaine;
And <u>Hubert</u> posting to returne those Lords,
Who deemd him dead, and parted discontent:
<u>Arthur</u> himselfe begins our latter Act,   10
Our Act of outrage, desprate furie, death;
Wherein fond rashnes murdreth first a Prince,
And Monkish falsnes poysneth last a King.
First Scene shews <u>Arthurs</u> death in infancie,
And last concludes <u>Johns</u> fatall tragedie.   15

The second part of the troublesome Raigne of King   IIA3
John, containing the entraunce of Lewes the French
Kings sonne: with the poysoning of King John by a Monke.
Scene ix

Enter yong Arthur on the walls.

Arthur

Now helpe good hap to further mine entent,

Crosse not my youth with any more extreames:

I venter life to gaine my libertie,

And if I die, worlds troubles have an end.

Feare gins disswade the strength of my resolve,   5

My holde will faile, and then alas I fall,

And if I fall, no question death is next:

Better desist, and live in prison still.

Prison said I? nay rather death than so:

Comfort and courage come againe to me.   10

Ile venter sure: tis but a leape for life.

He leapes, and brusing his bones, after he wakes from his
traunce, speakes thus;

Hoe, who is nigh? some bodie take me up.

Where is my mother? let me speake with her.

Who hurts me thus? speake hoe, where are you gone?

Ay me poore Arthur, I am here alone.   15

Why cald I mother, how did I forget?

My fall, my fall, hath kilde my Mothers Sonne.

How will she weepe at tidings of my death?

My death indeed, O God my bones are burst.

Sweete Jesu save my soule, forgive my rash attempt,   IIA3^V

Comfort my Mother, shield her from despaire,   21

When she shall heare my tragick overthrowe.

My heart controules the office of my toong,

My vitall powers forsake my brused trunck,

I dye I dye, heaven take my fleeting soule,   25

And Lady Mother all good hap to thee.   He dyes.

       Enter Penbrooke, Salsburie, Essex.

Essex

My Lords of Penbroke and of Salsbury

We must be carefull in our pollicie

To undermine the kepers of this place,

Else shall we never find the Princes grave.   30

Pembrooke

My Lord of Essex take no care for that,

I warrant you it was not closely done.

But who is this? lo Lords the withered flowre

Who in his life shinde like the Mornings blush,

Cast out a doore, denide his buriall right,   35

A pray for birds and beasts to gorge upon.

Salisbury

O ruthfull spectacle, O damned deede;

My sinnewes shake, my very heart doth bleede.

Essex

Leave childish teares brave Lords of England,

If waterfloods could fetch his life againe,   40

My eyes should conduit foorth a sea of teares.

If sobbs would helpe, or sorrowes serve the turne,

My heart should volie out deepe piercing plaints.

But bootlesse wert to breath as many sighes

As might eclipse the brightest Sommers sunne,   45

Heere rests the helpe, a service to his ghost.

Let not the tyrant causer of this dole,

Live to triumph in ruthfull massacres,

Give hand and hart, and Englishmen to armes,

Tis Gods decree to wreake us of these harmes.   50

Pembrooke

The best advise: But who commes posting heere.

Hubert

Right noble Lords, I speake unto you all,

The King intreates your soonest speed

To visit him, who on your present want,

Did ban and cursse his birth, himselfe and me,   55

For executing of his strict commaund.

I saw his passion, and at fittest time,

Assurde him of his cousins being safe,

Whome pittie would not let me doo to death,

He craves your company my Lords in haste,   60

To whome I will conduct young Arthur streight,

Who is in health under my custodie.

Essex

In health base villaine, wert not I leave thy crime

To Gods revenge, to whome revenge belongs,

Heere shouldst thou perish on my Rapires point.   65

Calst thou this health? such health betide thy friends,

And all that are of thy condition.

Hubert

My Lords, but heare me speake, and kill me then.

If heere I left not this yong Prince alive,

Maugre the hasty Edict of the King,   70

Who gave me charge to put out both his eyes,

That God that gave me living to this howre,

Thunder revenge upon me in this place:

And as I tenderd him with earnest love,

So God love me, and then I shall be well.   75

Salisbury

Hence traytor hence thy councel is heerein.   Exit Hubert.

Some in this place appoynted by the King

Have throwne him from this lodging here above,

And sure the murther hath bin newly done,

For yet the body is not fully colde.   80

Essex

How say you Lords, shall we with speed dispatch

Under our hands a packet into Fraunce

To bid the Dolphin enter with his force

To claime the Kingdome for his proper right,

His title maketh lawfull strength thereto.   85

Besides the Pope, on perill of his cursse,

Hath bard us of obedience unto <u>John</u>,   IIA4^v

This hatefull murder, <u>Lewes</u> his true discent,

The holy charge that wee receivde from <u>Rome</u>,

Are weightie reasons if you like my reede,   90

To make us all persever in this deede.

<u>Pembrooke</u>

My Lord of <u>Essex</u>, well have you advisde,

I will accord to further you in this.

<u>Salisbury</u>

And <u>Salsbury</u> will not gainsay the same.

But aid that course as far foorth as he can.   95

<u>Essex</u>

Then each of us send straight to his Allyes.

To winne them to this famous enterprise,

And let us all yclad in Palmers weede,

The tenth of April at Saint <u>Edmonds</u> <u>Bury</u>

Meete to confer, and on the Altar there   100

Sweare secrecie and aid to this advise.

Meane while let us conveigh this body hence,

And give him buriall as befits his state,

Keeping his months minde and his obsequies

With solemne intercession for his soule.   105

How say you Lordings, are you all agreed?

Pembrooke

The tenth of Aprill at Saint Edmonds Bury

God letting not, I will not faile the time.

Essex

Then let us all convey the body hence.

Exeunt, bearing Arthurs body.

Scene x

Enter King John with two or three and the Prophet.

K. John

Disturbed thoughts, foredoomers of mine ill,

Distracted passions, signes of growing harmes,

Strange Prophecies of imminent mishaps,

Confound my wits, and dull my senses so,

That every object these mine eyes behold   5

Seeme instruments to bring me to my end.

Ascension day is come, John feare not then

The prodigies this pratling Prophet threates.

Tis come indeede: ah were it fully past,

Then were I careles of a thousand feares.   10

The Diall tells me, it is twelve at noone.   IIB1
Were twelve at midnight past, then might I vaunt
False seers prophecies of no import.
Could I as well with this right hand of mine
Remove the Sunne from our Meridian,   15
Unto the noonstead circle of thantipodes,
As turne this steele from twelve to twelve agen,
Then John the date of fatall prophecies
Should with the Prophets life together end.
But Multa cadunt inter calicem supremaque labra.   20
Peter, unsay thy foolish doting dreame,
And by the Crowne of England heere I sweare,
To make thee great, and greatest of thy kin.

Peter

King John, although the time I have prescribed
Be but twelve houres remayning yet behinde,   25
Yet do I know by inspiration,
Ere that fixt time be fully come about,
King John shall not be King as heeretofore.

K. John

    Vain buzzard, what mischaunce can chaunce so soone

    To set a King beside his regall seate: 30

    My heart is good, my body passing strong,

    My land in peace, my enemies subdewd,

    Only my Barons storme at Arthurs death,

    But Arthur lives, I there the challenge growes,

    Were he dispatcht unto his longest home,   35

    Then were the King secure of thousand foes.

                  Enter Hubert.

    Hubert what news with thee, where are my Lords?

Hubert

    Hard newes my Lord, Arthur the lovely Prince

    Seeking to escape over the Castle walles,

    Fell headlong downe, and in the cursed fall   40

    He brake his bones, and there before the gate

    Your Barons found him dead, and breathlesse quite.

K. John

    Is Arthur dead?

    Then Hubert without more words hang the Prophet.

    Away with Peter, villen out of my sight,   45

    I am deafe, be gone, let him not speake a word.--

                 Exeunt Hubert and Peter.

Now John, thy feares are vanisht into smoake,   IIB1^v

Arthur is dead, thou guiltlesse of his death.

Sweete Youth, but that I strived for a Crowne,

I could have well affoorded to thine age   50

Long life, and happines to thy content.--

                  Enter the Bastard.

Philip, what newes with thee?

Bastard

    The newes I heard was Peters prayers,

    Who wisht like fortune to befall us all:

    And with that word, the rope his latest friend,   55

    Kept him from falling headlong to the ground.

K. John

    There let him hang, and be the Ravens food,

    While John triumphs in spight of Prophecies.

    But whats the tidings from the Popelings now.

    What say the Monkes and Priests to our proceedings?   60

    Or wheres the Barons that so sodainly

    Did leave the King upon a false surmise?

Bastard

    The Prelates storme and thirst for sharpe revenge.

    But please your Majestie, were that the worst,

    It little skild: a greater danger growes,   65

    Which must be weeded out by carefull speede,

    Or all is lost, for all is leveld at.

K. John

    More frights and feares, what ere thy tidings be,

    I am preparde: then Philip quickly say,

    Meane they to murder, or imprison me,   70

    To give my crowne away to Rome or Fraunce;

    Or will they each of them become a King?

    Worse than I thinke it is, it cannot be.

Bastard

    Not worse my Lord, but everie whit as bad.

    The Nobles have elected Lewes King,   75

    In right of Ladie Blanche your Neece, his Wife:

    His landing is expected every hower,

    The Nobles, Commons, Clergie, all Estates,

    Incited chiefely by the Cardinall,

<u>Pandulph</u> that lies here Legate for the Pope,   IIB2   80

Thinks long to see their new elected King.

And for undoubted proofe, see here my Liege

Letters to me from your Nobilitie,

To be a partie in this action:

Who under show of fained holines,   85

Appoynt their meeting at <u>S</u>. <u>Edmonds Bury,</u>

There to consult, conspire, and conclude

The overthrow and downfall of your State.

<u>K</u>. <u>John</u>

Why so it must be: one hower of content

Matcht with a month of passionate effects.   90

Why shines the Sunne to favour this consort?

Why doo the windes not breake their brazen gates,

And scatter all these perjurd complices,

With all their counsells and their damned drifts.

But see the welkin rolleth gently on,   95

Theres not a lowring clowde to frowne on them;

The heaven, the earth, the sunne, the moone and all

Conspire with those confederates my decay.

Then hell for me if any power be there,

Forsake that place, and guide me step by step   100

To poyson, strangle, murder in their steps

These traitors: oh that name is too good for them,

And death is easie: is there nothing worse

To wreake me on this proud peace-breaking crew?

What saist thou <u>Philip?</u> why assists thou not?   105

Bastard

   These curses (good my Lord) fit not the season:

   Help must descend from heaven against this treason.

<u>K</u>. John

   Nay thou wilt proove a traitor with the rest,

   Goe get thee to them, shame come to you all.

Bastard

   I would be loath to leave your Highnes thus,   110

   Yet you command, and I though grievd will goe.

<u>K</u>. John

   Ah <u>Philip</u> whether goest thou, come againe.

Bastard

   My Lord:

   These motions are as passions of a mad man.

<u>K</u>. John

   A mad man <u>Philip,</u> I am mad indeed,   115

   My hart is mazd, my senses all foredone.

And <u>John</u> of <u>England</u> now is quite undone.   IIB2^V

Was ever King as I opprest with cares?

Dame <u>Elianor</u> my noble Mother Queene,

My onely hope and comfort in distresse,   120

Is dead, and <u>England</u> excommunicate,

And I am interdicted by the Pope,

All Churches curst, their doores are sealed up,

And for the pleasure of the Romish Priest,

The service of the Highest is neglected;   125

The multitude (a beast of many heads)

Doo wish confusion to their Soveraigne;

The Nobles blinded with ambitions fumes,

Assemble powers to beat mine Empire downe,

And more than this, elect a forren King.   130

O <u>England</u>, wert thou ever miserable,

King <u>John</u> of <u>England</u> sees thee miserable:

<u>John</u>, tis thy sinnes that makes it miserable,

<u>Quicquid</u> <u>delirant</u> <u>Reges</u>, <u>plectuntur</u> <u>Achivi</u>.

<u>Philip</u>, as thou hast ever lovde thy King,   135

So show it now: post to S. Edmonds Bury,

Dissemble with the Nobles, know their drifts,

Confound their divelish plots, and damnd devices.

Though John be faultie, yet let subjects beare,

He will amend and right the peoples wrongs.   140

A Mother though she were unnaturall,

Is better than the kindest Stepdame is:

Let never Englishman trust forraine rule.

Then Philip shew thy fealtie to thy King,

And mongst the Nobles plead thou for the King.   145

Bastard

I goe my Lord:--see how he is distraught,

This is the cursed Priest of Italy

Hath heapt these mischiefes on this haplesse Land.

Now Philip, hadst thou Tullyes eloquence,

Then mightst thou hope to plead with good successe.-- 150

                                                         Exit.

K. John

And art thou gone? successe may follow thee:

Thus hast thou shewd thy kindnes to thy King.--

Sirra, in hast goe greete the Cardinall,   IIB3
Pandulph I meane, the Legate from the Pope.
Say that the King desires to speake with him.--   155

                                    Exit Attendant.

Now John bethinke thee how thou maist resolve:
And if thou wilt continue Englands King,
Then cast about to keepe thy Diadem;
For life and land, and all is leveld at.
The Pope of Rome, tis he that is the cause,   160
He curseth thee, he sets thy subjects free
From due obedience to their Soveraigne:
He animates the Nobles in their warres,
He gives away the Crowne to Philips Sonne,
And pardons all that seeke to murther thee: 165
And thus blinde zeale is still predominant.
Then John there is no way to keepe thy Crowne,
But finely to dissemble with the Pope:
That hand that gave the wound must give the salve
To cure the hurt, els quite incurable.   170

Thy sinnes are farre too great to be the man

T'abolish Pope, and Popery from thy Realme:

But in thy Seate, if I may gesse at all,

A King shall raigne that shall suppresse them all.

Peace John, here comes the Legate of the Pope,   175

Dissemble thou, and whatsoere thou saist,

Yet with thy heart wish their confusion.--

Enter Pandulph.

Pandulph

Now John, unworthie man to breath on earth,

That dost oppugne against thy Mother Church:

Why am I sent for to thy cursed selfe?   180

K. John

Thou man of God, Vicegerent for the Pope,

The holy Vicar of S. Peters Church,

Upon my knees, I pardon crave of thee,

And doo submit me to the sea of Rome,

And vow for penaunce of my high offence,   185

To take on me the holy Crosse of Christ,   IIB3^V

And cary Armes in holy Christian warres.

Pandulph

No **John**, thy crowching and dissembling thus

Cannot deceive the Legate of the Pope,

Say what thou wilt, I will not credit thee: 190

Thy Crowne and Kingdome both are tane away,

And thou art curst without redemption.

K. John

--Accurst indeede to kneele to such a drudge,

And get no help with thy submission,

Unsheath thy sword, and sley the misprowd Priest   195

That thus triumphs ore thee a mighty King:

No **John** submit againe dissemble yet,

For Priests and Women must be flattered.--

Yet holy Father thou thy selfe dost know

No time to late for sinners to repent,   200

Absolve me then, and **John** doth sweare to doo

The uttermost what ever thou demaundst.

Pandulph

    John, now I see thy harty penitence,

    I rew and pitty thy distrest estate,

    One way is left to reconcile thy selfe,   205

    And only one which I shall shew to thee.

    Thou must surrender to the sea of Rome

    Thy Crowne and Diademe, then shall the Pope

    Defend thee from thinvasion of thy foes.

    And where his holinesse hath kindled Fraunce,   210

    And set thy subjects hearts at warre with thee,

    Then shall he cursse thy foes, and beate them downe,

    That seeke the discontentment of the King.

K. John

    --From bad to woorse: or I must loose my realme,

    Or give my Crowne for pennance unto Rome?   215

    A miserie more piercing than the darts

    That breake from burning exhalations power.

    What? shall I give my Crowne with this right hand?

    No: with this hand defend thy Crowne and thee.--

              Enter Messenger.

What newes with thee.   220

<u>Messenger</u>   IIB4

Please it your Majestie, there is descried on the Coast of

Kent an hundred Sayle of Ships, which of all men is

thought to be the French Fleete, under the conduct of the

Dolphin, so that it puts the Cuntrie in a mutinie, so they

send to your Grace for succour.   225

<u>K</u>. John

How now Lord Cardinall, whats your best advise,

These mutinies must be allayd in time

By pollicy or headstrong rage at least.--

O John, these troubles tyre thy wearyed soule,

And like to Luna in a sad Eclipse,   230

So are thy thoughts and passions for this newes.

Well may it be when Kings are grieved so,

The vulgar sort worke Princes overthrow.--

<u>Pandulph</u>

K. John,

For not effecting of thy plighted vow,   235

This strange annoyance happens to thy land:

But yet be reconcild unto the Church,

And nothing shall be grievous to thy state.

K. John

    On Pandulph be it as thou hast decreed,

    John will not spurne against thy sound advise,   240

    Come lets away, and with thy helpe I trow

    My Realme shall florish and my Crowne in peace.   Exeunt.

    Scene xi

    Enter the Nobles, Penbrooke, Essex, Salisbury, Bewchampe,

    with others.

Pembrooke

    Now sweet S. Edmond holy Saint in heaven,

    Whose Shrine is sacred, high esteemd on earth,

    Infuse a constant zeale in all our hearts

    To prosecute this act of mickle waight,

    Lord Bewchampe say, what friends have you procurde.   5

Bewchampe

    The L. FitzWater, L. Percy, and L. Rosse,

    Vowd meeting heere this day the leventh houre.

Essex

    Under the cloke of holie Pilgrimage,

By that same houre on warrant of their faith,   IIB4v

Phillip Plantagenet, a bird of swiftest wing,   10

Lord Eustace Vescy, Lord Cressy, and Lord Mowbrey,

Appoynted meeting at S. Edmonds Shrine.

Pembrooke

Untill their presence ile conceale my tale,

Sweete complices in holie Christian acts,

That venture for the purchase of renowne,   15

Thrice welcome to the league of high resolve,

That pawne their bodies for their soules regard.

Essex

Now wanteth but the rest to end this worke,

In Pilgrims habit commes our holie troupe

A furlong hence with swift unwonted pace,   20

May be they are the persons you exspect.

Pembrooke

With swift unwonted gate, see what a thing is zeale,

That spurrs them on with fervence to this Shrine,

Now joy come to them for their true intent

And in good time heere come the warmen all   25

That sweate in body by the minds disease

        Enter the Bastard Phillip, Percy, etc.

Hap and hartsease brave Lordings be your lot.

Bastard

Amen my Lords, the like betide your lucke,

And all that travaile in a Christian cause.

Essex

Cheerely replied brave braunch of kingly stock,   30

A right <u>Plantaginet</u> should reason so.

But silence Lords, attend our commings cause,

The servile yoke that payned us with toyle,

On strong instinct hath framd this conventickle,

To ease our necks of servitudes contempt.   35

Should I not name the foeman of our rest,

Which of you all so barraine in conceipt,

As cannot levell at the man I meane?

But least Enigmas shadow shining truth

Plainely to paint as truth requires no arte,   40

Theffect of this resort importeth this,

To roote and cleane extirpate tirant <u>John,</u>

Tirant I say, appealing to the man.

(If any heere) that loves him, and I aske   IIC1
What kindship, lenitie, or christian raigne   45
Rules in the man, to barre this foule impeach.
First I inferre the <u>Chesters</u> bannishment:
For reprehending him in most unchristian crimes,
Was speciall notice of a tyrants will.
But were this all, the devill should be savd,   50
But this the least of many thousand faults,
That circumstance with leisure might display.
Our private wrongs, no parcell of my tale
Which now in presence, but for some great cause
Might wish to him as to a mortall foe.   55
But shall I close the period with an acte
Abhorring in the eares of Christian men,
His Cosens death, that sweet unguilty childe,
Untimely butcherd by the tyrants meanes,
Heere is my proofes as cleere as gravell brooke,   60
And on the same I further must inferre,

That who upholds a tyrant in his course,

Is culpable of all his damned guilt.

To show the which, is yet to be describd.

My Lord of Penbrooke shew what is behinde,   65

Only I say that were there nothing else

To move us but the Popes most dreadfull cursse,

Whereof we are assured if we fayle,

It were inough to instigate us all

With earnestnesse of sprit to seeke a meane   70

To dispossesse John of his regiment.

Pembrooke

Well hath my Lord of Essex tolde his tale,

Which I aver for most substanciall truth,

And more to make the matter to our minde,

I say that Lewes in chalenge of his wife,   75

Hath title of an uncontrouled plea

To all that longeth to our English Crowne.

Short tale to make, the Sea apostolick

Hath offerd dispensation for the fault,

If any be, as trust me none I know   IIC1^v   80

By planting <u>Lewes</u> in the Usurpers roome:

This is the cause of all our presence heere,

That on the holie Altar we protest

To ayde the right of <u>Lewes</u> with goods and life,

Who on our knowledge is in Armes for <u>England.</u>   85

What say you Lords?

<u>Salisbury</u>

As <u>Pembrooke</u> sayth, affirmeth <u>Salsburie:</u>

Faire <u>Lewes</u> of <u>Fraunce</u> that spoused Lady <u>Blanch,</u>

Hath title of an uncontrouled strength

To <u>England,</u> and what longeth to the Crowne: 90

In right whereof, as we are true informd,

The Prince is marching hitherward in Armes.

Our purpose to conclude that with a word,

Is to invest him as we may devise,

King of our Countrey in the tyrants stead: 95

And so the warrant on the Altar sworne,

And so the intent for which we hither came.

Bastard

    My Lord of <u>Salsbury,</u> I cannot couch

    My speeches with the needfull words of arte,

    As doth beseeme in such a waightie worke,   100

    But what my conscience and my dutie will

    I purpose to impart.

    For <u>Chesters</u> exile, blame his busie wit,

    That medled where his dutie quite forbade:

    For any private causes that you have,   105

    Me thinke they should not mount to such a height,

    As to depose a King in their revenge.

    For <u>Arthurs</u> death King <u>John</u> was innocent,

    He desperat was the deathsman to himselfe,

    Which you to make a colour to your crime   110

    Injustly do impute to his default,

    But where fell traytorisme hath residence,

    There wants no words to set despight on worke.

    I say tis shame, and worthy all reproofe,

    To wrest such pettie wrongs in tearmes of right,   115

    Against a King annoynted by the Lord.

Why Salsburie admit the wrongs are true,   IIC2
Yet subjects may not take in hand revenge,
And rob the heavens of their proper power,
Where sitteth he to whome revenge belongs.   120
And doth a Pope, a Priest, a man of pride
Give charters for the lives of lawfull Kings?
What can he blesse, or who regards his cursse,
But such as give to man, and takes from God.
I speake it in the sight of God above,   125
Theres not a man that dyes in your beliefe,
But sels his soule perpetually to payne.
Ayd Lewes, leave God, kill John, please hell,
Make havock of the welfare of your soules,
For heere I leave you in the sight of heaven,   130
A troupe of traytors foode for hellish feends;
If you desist, then follow me as friends,
If not, then doo your worst as hatefull traytors.
For Lewes his right alas tis too too lame,
A senselesse clayme, if truth be titles friend.   135

In briefe, if this be cause of our resort,

Our Pilgrimage is to the Devils Shrine.

I came not Lords to troup as traytors doo,

Nor will I counsaile in so bad a cause:

Please you returne, wee go againe as friends,   140

If not, I to my King, and you where traytors please. <u>Exit</u>.

Percy

A hote young man, and so my Lords proceed,

I let him go, and better lost then found.

Pembrooke

What say you Lords, will all the rest proceed,

Will you all with me sweare upon the Aulter   145

That you wil to the death be ayd to <u>Lewes,</u>

And enemy to <u>John?</u> Every man lay his hand

By mine, in witnes of his harts accord.

Well then, every man to Armes to meete the King

Who is alreadie before <u>London</u>.   150

<u>Messenger</u> <u>Enter</u>.

What newes Harrold.

Messenger   IIC2^v

    The right Christian Prince my Maister, <u>Lewes</u> of <u>Fraunce</u>,

is at hand, comming to visit your Honors, directed hether

by the right honorable <u>Richard</u> Earle of <u>Bigot</u>, to conferre

with your Honors.   155

Pembrooke

    How neere is his Highnesse?

Messenger

    Ready to enter your presence.

        <u>Enter</u> Lewes, <u>Earle</u> Bigot, Melun, <u>with his troupe</u>.

Lewes

    Faire Lords of <u>England</u>, <u>Lewes</u> salutes you all

As friends, and firme welwillers of his weale,

At whose request from plenty flowing <u>Fraunce</u>   160

Crossing the Ocean with a Southern gale,

He is in person come at your commaunds

To undertake and gratifie withall

The fulnesse of your favours proffred him.

But worlds brave men, omitting promises,   165

Till time be minister of more amends,

I must acquaint you with our fortunes course.

The heavens dewing favours on my head,

Have in their conduct safe with victorie,

Brought me along your well manured bounds,   170

With small repulse, and little crosse of chaunce.

Your Citie Rochester with great applause

By some devine instinct layd armes aside:

And from the hollow holes of Thamesis

Eccho apace replide Vive le roy.   175

From thence, along the wanton rowling glade

To Troynovant your fayre Metropolis,

With luck came Lewes to shew his troupes of Fraunce,

Waving our Ensignes with the dallying windes,

The fearefull object of fell frowning warre;   180

Where after some assault, and small defence,

Heavens may I say, and not my warlike troupe,

Temperd their hearts to take a friendly foe

Within the compasse of their high built walles,

Geving me title as it seemd they wish.   185

Thus Fortune (Lords) acts to your forwardnes   IIC3

Meanes of content in lieu of former griefe:

And may I live but to requite you all,

Worlds wish were mine in dying noted yours.

Salisbury

Welcome the balme that closeth up our wounds,   190

The soveraigne medcine for our quick recure,

The anchor of our hope, the onely prop,

Whereon depends our lives, our lands, our weale,

Without the which, as sheepe without their heard,

(Except a shepheard winking at the wolfe)   195

We stray, we pine, we run to thousand harmes.

No mervaile then though with unwonted joy

We welcome him that beateth woes away.

Lewes

Thanks to you all of this religious league,

A holy knot of Catholique consent.   200

I cannot name you Lordings, man by man,

But like a stranger unacquainted yet,

In generall I promise faithfull love:

Lord Bigot, brought me to S. <u>Edmonds</u> Shrine,

Giving me warrant of a Christian oath,   205

That this assembly came devoted heere,

To sweare according as your packets showd,

Homage and loyall service to our selfe,

I neede not doubt the suretie of your wills;

Since well I know for many of your sakes   210

The townes have yeelded on their owne accords:

Yet for a fashion, not for misbeliefe,

My eyes must witnes, and these eares must heare

Your oath upon the holy Altar sworne,

And after march to end our commings cause.   215

<u>Salisbury</u>

That we intend no other than good truth,

All that are present of this holy League,

For confirmation of our better trust,

In presence of his Highnes sweare with me,

The sequel that my selfe shal utter heere.   220

I <u>Thomas</u> <u>Plantaginet</u> Earle of <u>Salisbury,</u> sweare   IIC3^v

upon the Altar, and by the holy Armie of Saints, homage

and alleagance to the right Christian Prince <u>Lewes</u> of

<u>Fraunce,</u> as true and rightfull King to <u>England,</u> <u>Cornwall</u>

and <u>Wales,</u> and to their Territories, in the defence   225

whereof I uppon the holy Altare sweare all forwardnes.

<u>All</u> <u>the</u> <u>Eng</u>. <u>Lords</u> <u>sweare,</u>

As the noble Earle hath sworne, so sweare we all.

Lewes

I rest assured on your holy oath,

And on this Altar in like sort I sweare

Love to you all, and Princely recompence   230

To guerdon your goodwills unto the full.

And since I am at this religious Shrine,

My good welwillers, give us leave awhile

To use some orisons our selves apart

To all the holy companie of heaven,   235

That they will smile upon our purposes,

And bring them to a fortunate event.

Salisbury

We leave your Highnes to your good intent.

<u>Exeunt</u> <u>Lords</u> <u>of</u> England.

Lewes

Now Vicount <u>Meloun,</u> what remaines behinde?

Trust me these traitors to their sovereigne State   240

Are not to be beleevde in any sort.

Melun

Indeed my Lord, they that infringe their oaths,

And play the rebells gainst their native King,

Will for as little cause revolt from you,

If ever opportunitie incite them so: 245

For once forsworne, and never after sound,

Theres no affiance after perjurie.

Lewes

Well <u>Meloun</u> well, lets smooth with them awhile,

Untill we have asmuch as they can doo:

And when their vertue is exhaled drie,   250

Ile hang them for the guerdon of their help,

Meane while wee'l use them as a precious poyson

To undertake the issue of our hope.

French Lord

Tis policie (my Lord) to bait our hookes

With merry smiles, and promise of much waight: 255

But when your Highnes needeth them no more,   IIC4

Tis good make sure work with them, least indeede

They proove to you as to their naturall King.

Melun

Trust me my Lord, right well have you advisde

Venyme for use, but never for a sport   260

Is to be dallyed with, least it infect.

Were you instald, as soone I hope you shall:

Be free from traitors, and dispatch them all.

Lewes

That so I meane, I sweare before you all

On this same Altar, and by heavens power,   265

Theres not an English traytor of them all,

John once dispatcht, and I faire Englands King,

Shall on his shoulders beare his head one day,

But I will crop it for their guilts desert:

Nor shall their heires enjoy their Signories,   270

But perish by their parents fowle amisse.

This have I sworne, and this will I performe,

If ere I come unto the height I hope.

Lay downe your hands, and sweare the same with mee.

<u>The French Lords sweare</u>.

Why so, now call them in, and speake them faire,   275

A smile of <u>France</u> will feed an English foole.

Beare them in hand as friends, for so they be:

But in the hart like traytors as they are.

<u>Enter the English Lords</u>.

Now famous followers, chieftaines of the world,

Have we sollicited with heartie prayer   280

The heaven in favour of our high attempt.

Leave we this place, and march we with our power

To rowse the Tyrant from his chiefest hold:

And when our labours have a prosprous end,

Each man shall reape the fruite of his desert.   285

And so resolvde, brave followers let us hence.   <u>Exeunt</u>.

Scene xii   IIC4^v

Enter <u>K</u>. John, <u>Bastard,</u> Pandulph, <u>and</u> <u>a</u> <u>many priests</u>
<u>with</u> <u>them.</u>

<u>Pandulph</u>

    Thus <u>John</u> thou art absolvde from all thy sinnes,

    And freed by order from our Fathers curse.

    Receive thy Crowne againe, with this proviso,

    That thou remaine true liegeman to the Pope,

    And carry armes in right of holy <u>Rome</u>.   5

<u>K</u>. John

    I holde the same as tenaunt to the Pope,

    And thanke your Holines for your kindnes showne.

<u>Bastard</u>

    --A proper jest, when Kings must stoop to Friers,

    Neede hath no law, when Friers must be Kings.--

              <u>Enter</u> <u>a</u> <u>Messenger.</u>

<u>Messenger</u>

    Please it your Majestie, the Prince of <u>Fraunce,</u>   10

With all the Nobles of your Graces Land,

Are marching hetherward in good aray.

Where ere they set their foote, all places yeeld:

Thy Land is theirs, and not a foote holds out

But <u>Dover</u> Castle, which is hard besiegd.   15

<u>Pandulph</u>

Feare not King <u>John,</u> thy kingdome is the popes,

And they shall know his Holines hath power,

To beate them soone from whence he hath to doo.

<u>Drums</u> <u>and</u> <u>Trumpets</u>. <u>Enter</u> Lewes, Melun, Salisbury, Essex,

Pembrooke, <u>and</u> <u>all</u> <u>the</u> <u>Nobles</u> <u>from</u> Fraunce, <u>and</u> England.

<u>Lewes</u>

<u>Pandulph,</u> as gave his Holines in charge,

So hath the <u>Dolphin</u> mustred up his troupes   20

And wonne the greatest part of all this Land.

But ill becomes your Grace Lord Cardinall,

Thus to converse with <u>John</u> that is accurst.

Pandulph   IID1

    Lewes of France, victorious Conqueror,

    Whose sword hath made this Iland quake for fear;   25

    Thy forwardnes to fight for holy Rome,

    Shalbe remunerated to the full:

    But know my Lord, K. John is now absolvde,

    The Pope is pleasde, the Land is blest agen,

    And thou hast brought each thing to good effect.   30

    It resteth then that thou withdraw thy powers,

    And quietly returne to Fraunce againe:

    For all is done the Pope would wish thee doo.

Lewes

    But als not done that Lewes came to doo.

    Why Pandulph, hath K. Philip sent his sonne   35

    And been at such excessive charge in warres,

    To be dismist with words? K. John shall know,

    England is mine, and he usurps my right.

Pandulph

    Lewes, I charge thee and thy complices

    Upon the paine of Pandulphs holy curse,   40

    That thou withdraw thy powers to Fraunce againe,

    And yeeld up London and the neighbour Townes

    That thou hast tane in England by the sword.

Melun

    Lord Cardinall, by Lewes princely leave,

    It can be nought but usurpation   45

    In thee, the Pope, and all the Church of Rome,

    Thus to insult on Kings of Christendome,

    Now with a word to make them carie armes,

    Then with a word to make them leave their armes.

    This must not be:--Prince Lewes keepe thine owne,   50

    Let Pope and Popelings curse their bellyes full.

Bastard

    My Lord of Melun, what title had the Prince

    To England and the Crowne of Albion,

    But such a title as the Pope confirmde:

    The Prelate now lets fall his fained claime: 55

    Lewes is but the agent for the Pope,

    Then must the Dolphin cease, sith he hath ceast:

    But cease or no, it greatly matters not,

    If you my Lords and Barrons of the Land

Will leave the French, and cleave unto your King.   IID1^V

For shame ye Peeres of England, suffer not   61

Your selves, your honours, and your land to fall:

But with resolved thoughts beate back the French,

And free the Land from yoke of servitude.

Salisbury

Philip, not so, Lord Lewes is our King,   65

And we will follow him unto the death.

Pandulph

Then in the name of Innocent the Pope,

I curse the Prince and all that take his part,

And excommunicate the rebell Peeres

As traytors to the King, and to the Pope.   70

Lewes

Pandolph, our swords shall blesse our selves agen:

Prepare thee John, Lords follow me your King.

Exeunt Lewes and his followers.

K. John

—Accursed John, the divell owes thee shame,

Resisting Rome, or yeelding to the Pope, alls one.

The divell take the Pope, the Peeres, and Fraunce: 75

Shame be my share for yeelding to the Priest.—

Pandulph

    Comfort thy self K. John, the Cardnall goes

    Upon his curse to make them leave their armes.   Exit.

Bastard

    Comfort my Lord, and curse the Cardinall,

    Betake your self to armes, my troupes are prest   80

    To answere Lewes with a lustie shocke:

    The English Archers have their quivers full,

    Their bowes are bent, the pykes are prest to push:

    God cheere my Lord, K. Richards fortune hangs

    Upon the plume of warlike Philips helme.   85

    Then let them know his brother and his sonne

    Are leaders of the Englishmen at armes.

K. John

    Philip I know not how to answere thee:

    But let us hence, to answere Lewes pride.   Exeunt.

    Excursions. Enter Meloun with English Lords, Salisbury

    and Pembrooke.

Melun

    O I am slaine, Nobles, Salsbury, Pembrooke,   90

    My soule is charged, heare me: for what I say

    Concernes the Peeres of England, and their State.

Listen, brave Lords, a fearfull mourning tale   IID2
To be delivered by a man of death.
Behold these scarres, the dole of bloudie Mars   95
Are harbingers from natures common foe,
Cyting this trunke to Tellus prison house;
Lifes charter (Lordings) lasteth not an hower:
And fearfull thoughts, forerunners of my end,
Bids me give Phisicke to a sickly soule.   100
O Peeres of England, know you what you doo,
Theres but a haire that sunders you from harme,
The hooke is bayted, and the traine is made,
And simply you runne doating to your deaths.
But least I dye, and leave my tale untolde,   105
With silence slaughtering so brave a crew,
This I averre, if Lewes win the day,
Theres not an Englishman that lifts his hand
Against King John to plant the heire of Fraunce,
But is already damnd to cruell death.   110

I heard it vowd; my selfe amongst the rest
Swore on the Altar aid to this Edict.
Two causes Lords, makes me display this drift,
The greatest for the freedome of my soule,
That longs to leave this mansion free from guilt: 115
The other on a naturall instinct,
For that my Grandsire was an Englishman.
Misdoubt not Lords the truth of my discourse,
No frenzie, nor no brainsick idle fit,
But well advisde, and wotting what I say,   120
Pronounce I here before the face of heaven,
That nothing is discovered but a truth.
Tis time to flie, submit your selves to John,
The smiles of Fraunce shade in the frownes of death,
Lift up your swords, turne face against the French,   125
Expell the yoke thats framed for your necks.
Back warmen, back, imbowell not the clyme,
Your seate, your nurse, your birth dayes breathing place,

That bred you, beares you, brought you up in armes.   IID2^V
Ah be not so ingrate to digge your Mothers grave,   130
Preserve your lambes and beate away the Wolfe.
My soule hath said, contritions penitence
Layes hold on mans redemption for my sinne.
Farewell my Lords,
Witnes my faith when wee are met in heaven,   135
And for my kindnes give me grave roome heere.
My soule doth fleete, worlds vanities farewell.   <u>He dyes.</u>

<u>Salisbury</u>

Now joy betide thy soule wel-meaning man.
--How now my Lords, what cooling card is this,
A greater griefe growes now than earst hath been.   140
What counsell give you, shall we stay and dye?
Or shall we home, and kneele unto the King.

<u>Pembrooke</u>

My hart misgave this sad accursed newes:
What have we done, fie Lords, what frenzie moved
Our hearts to yeeld unto the pride of <u>Fraunce?</u>   145
If we persever, we are sure to dye:
If we desist, small hope againe of life.

Salisbury

    Beare hence the bodie of this wretched man,

    That made us wretched with his dying tale,

    And stand not wayling on our present harmes,   150

    As women wont: but seeke our harmes redresse.

    As for my selfe, I will in hast be gon:

    And kneele for pardon to our Sovereigne John.

Pembrooke

    I, theres the way, lets rather kneele to him,

    Than to the French that would confound us all.   155

                Exeunt bearing Meluns body.

    Scene xiii

        Enter King John carried betweene two Lords.

K. John

    Set downe, set downe the load not worth your pain,

    For done I am with deadly wounding griefe:

    Sickly and succourles, hopeles of any good,

    The world hath wearied me, and I have wearied it:

    It loaths I live, I live and loath my selfe.   5

    Who pities me? to whom have I been kinde?

    But to a few; a few will pitie me.

    Why dye I not? Death scornes so vilde a pray.

Why live I not, life hates so sad a prize.   IID3

I sue to both to be retaynd of either,   10

But both are deafe, I can be heard of neither.

Nor death nor life, yet life and neare the neere,

Ymixt with death biding I wot not where.

<u>Enter the Bastard.</u>

Bastard

How fares my Lord that he is caryed thus,

Not all the aukward fortunes yet befalne,   15

Made such impression of lament in me.

Nor ever did my eye attaynt my heart

With any object moving more remorse,

Than now beholding of a mighty King,

Borne by his Lords in such distressed state.   20

<u>K</u>. <u>John</u>

What news with thee, if bad, report it straite:

If good, be mute, it doth but flatter me.

Bastard

Such as it is, and heavie though it be

To glut the world with tragick elegies,

Once will I breath to agravate the rest,   25
Another moane to make the measure full.
The bravest bowman had not yet sent forth
Two arrowes from the quiver at his side,
But that a rumor went throughout our Campe,
That John was fled, the King had left the field.   30
At last the rumor scald these eares of mine,
Who rather chose as sacrifice for Mars,
Than ignominious scandall by retyre.
I cheerd the troupes as did the Prince of Troy
His weery followers gainst the Mirmidons,   35
Crying alowde S. George, the day is ours.
But feare had captivated courage quite,
And like the Lamb before the greedie Wolfe,
So hartlesse fled our warmen from the feeld.
Short tale to make, my selfe amongst the rest,   40
Was faine to flie before the eager foe.
By this time night had shadowed all the earth,
With sable curteines of the blackest hue,
And fenst us from the fury of the French,

As <u>Io</u> from the jealous <u>Junos</u> eye,   IID3^v   45
When in the morning our troupes did gather head,
Passing the washes with our carriages,
The impartiall tyde deadly and inexorable,
Came raging in with billowes threatning death,
And swallowed up the most of all our men,   50
My selfe upon a Galloway right free, well pacde,
Out stript the flouds that followed wave by wave,
I so escapt to tell this tragick tale.

<u>K</u>. <u>John</u>
Griefe upon griefe, yet none so great a griefe,
To end this life, and thereby rid my griefe.   55
Was ever any so infortunate,
The right Idea of a curssed man,
As I, poore I, a triumph for despight,
My fever growes, what ague shakes me so?
How farre to Swinsteed, tell me do you know,   60
Present unto the Abbot word of my repaire.
My sicknesse rages, to tirannize upon me,
I cannot live unlesse this fever leave me.

<u>Bastard</u>
Good cheare my Lord, the Abbey is at hand,
Behold my Lord the Churchmen come to meete you.   65

<u>Enter the Abbot, and certayne Monks</u>.

Abbot

   All health and happines to our soveraigne Lord the King.

K. John

   Nor health nor happines hath <u>John</u> at all.

   Say Abbot am I welcome to thy house.

Abbot

   Such welcome as our Abbey can affoord,

   Your Majesty shalbe assured of.   70

Bastard

   The King thou seest is weake and very faint,

   What victuals hast thou to refresh his Grace.

Abbot

   Good store my Lord, of that you neede not feare,

   For Lincolneshire, and these our Abbey grounds

   Were never fatter, nor in better plight.   75

K. John

   <u>Phillip,</u> thou never needst to doubt of cates,

   Nor King nor Lord is seated halfe so well,

   As are the Abbeys throughout all the land,

   If any plot of ground do passe another,

The Friers fasten on it streight: IID4   80
But let us in to taste of their repast,
It goes against my heart to feed with them,
Or be beholding to such Abbey groomes.   Exeunt.
                    Manet Thomas the Monke.

Thomas

Is this the King that never lovd a Frier?
Is this the man that doth contemne the Pope?   85
Is this the man that robd the holy Church,
And yet will flye unto a Friory?
Is this the King that aymes at Abbeys lands?
Is this the man whome all the world abhorres,
And yet will flye unto a Friory?   90
Accurst be Swinsteed Abbey, Abbot, Friers,
Moncks, Nuns, and Clarks, and all that dwells therein,
If wicked John escape alive away.
Now if that thou wilt looke to merit heaven,
And be canonizd for a holy Saint: 95
To please the world with a deserving worke,
Be thou the man to set thy cuntrey free,
And murder him that seekes to murder thee.

<u>Enter the Abbot unperceived.</u>

<u>Abbot</u>

Why are not you within to cheare the King?

He now begins to mend, and will to meate.   100

<u>Thomas</u>

What if I say to strangle him in his sleepe?

<u>Abbot</u>

What at thy <u>mumpsimus?</u> away,

And seeke some meanes for to pastime the King.

<u>Thomas</u>

Ile set a dudgeon dagger at his heart,

And with a mallet knock him on the head.   105

<u>Abbot</u>

Alas, what meanes this Monke to murther me?

Dare lay my life heel kill me for my place.

<u>Thomas</u>

Ile poyson him, and it shall neare be knowne,

And then shall I be chiefest of my house.

<u>Abbot</u>

If I were dead, indeed he is the next,   110

But ile away, for why the Monke is mad,

And in his madnesse he will murther me.

<u>Thomas</u>   IID4^V

My L.

I cry your Lordship mercy, I saw you not.

<u>Abbot</u>

Alas good <u>Thomas</u> doo not murther me,   115

And thou shalt have my place with thousand thanks.

<u>Thomas</u>

I murther you, God sheeld from such a thought.

<u>Abbot</u>

If thou wilt needes, yet let me say my prayers.

<u>Thomas</u>

I will not hurt your Lordship good my Lord:

But if you please, I will impart a thing   120

That shall be beneficiall to us all.

<u>Abbot</u>

Wilt thou not hurt me holy Monke, say on.

<u>Thomas</u>

You know my Lord the King is in our house.

<u>Abbot</u>

True.

<u>Thomas</u>

You know likewise the King abhors a Frier.   125

<u>Abbot</u>

True.

<u>Thomas</u>

And he that loves not a Frier is our enemy.

<u>Abbot</u>

Thou sayst true.

<u>Thomas</u>

Then the King is our enemy.

<u>Abbot</u>

True.   130

<u>Thomas</u>

Why then should we not kil our enemy, and the King being

our enemy, why then should we not kill the King.

<u>Abbot</u>

O blessed Monke, I see God moves thy minde

To free this land from tyrants slavery.

But who dare venter for to do this deede?   135

<u>Thomas</u>

Who dare? why I my Lord dare do the deede,

Ile free my Countrey and the Church from foes,

And merit heaven by killing of a King.

<u>Abbot</u>

<u>Thomas</u> kneele downe, and if thou art resolvde,

I will absolve thee heere from all thy sinnes,   140

For why the deede is meritorious.

Forward and feare not man, for every month,

Our Friers shall sing a Masse for <u>Thomas</u> soule.

<u>Thomas</u>

God and S. <u>Francis</u> prosper my attempt,

For now my Lord I goe about my worke.   <u>Exeunt.</u>   145

Scene xiv

Enter Lewes and his armie.

Lewes

Thus victory in bloudy Lawrell clad,

Followes the fortune of young Lodowicke,

The Englishmen as daunted at our sight,

Fall as the fowle before the Eagles eyes.   IIE1

Only two crosses of contrary change   5

Do nip my heart, and vexe me with unrest.

Lord Melons death, the one part of my soule,

A braver man did never live in Fraunce.

The other griefe, I thats a gall in deede,

To thinke that Dover Castell should hold out   10

Gainst all assaults, and rest impregnable.

Yee warlike race of Francus Hectors sonne,

Triumph in conquest of that tyrant John,

The better halfe of England is our owne,

And towards the conquest of the other part,   15

We have the face of all the English Lords,

What then remaines but overrun the land.

Be resolute my warlike followers,

And if good fortune serve as she begins,

The poorest peasant of the Realme of Fraunce   20

Shall be a maister ore an English Lord.

<u>Enter a Messenger.</u>

Fellow what newes.

Messenger

    Pleaseth your Grace, the Earle of <u>Salsbury,</u>

    <u>Penbroke,</u> <u>Essex,</u> <u>Clare,</u> and <u>Arundell,</u>

    With all the Barons that did fight for thee,   25

    Are on a suddeine fled with all their powers,

    To joyne with <u>John,</u> to drive thee back againe.

<u>Enter another Messenger.</u>

Messenger

    <u>Lewes</u> my Lord why standst thou in a maze,

    Gather thy troups, hope not of help from <u>Fraunce,</u>

    For all thy forces being fiftie sayle,   30

    Conteyning twenty thousand souldyers,

    With victuall and munition for the warre,

    Putting from <u>Callis</u> in unluckie time,

    Did crosse the seas, and on the <u>Goodwin</u> sands,

    The men, munition, and the ships are lost.   35

<u>Enter another Messenger.</u>

Lewes

    More newes? say on.

Messenger

    <u>John</u> (my Lord) with all his scattered troupes,

Flying the fury of your conquering sword,   IIE1^V

As <u>Pharaoh</u> earst within the bloody sea,

So he and his environed with the tyde,   40

On <u>Lincolne</u> washes all were overwhelmed,

The Barons fled, our forces cast away.

<u>Lewes</u>

Was ever heard such unexspected newes?

<u>Messenger</u>

Yet <u>Lodowike</u> revive thy dying heart,

King <u>John</u> and all his forces are consumde.   45

The lesse thou needst the ayd of English Earles,

The lesse thou needst to grieve thy Navies wracke,

And follow tymes advantage with successe.

<u>Lewes</u>

Brave <u>Frenchmen</u> armde with magnanimitie,

March after <u>Lewes</u> who will leade you on   50

To chase the Barons power that wants a head,

For <u>John</u> is drownd, and I am <u>Englands</u> King.

Though our munition and our men be lost,

<u>Phillip</u> of <u>Fraunce</u> will send us fresh supplyes.   <u>Exeunt.</u>

Scene xv

Enter <u>two</u> <u>Friers</u> <u>laying</u> <u>a</u> <u>Cloth.</u>

<u>1 Frier</u>

Dispatch, dispatch, the King desires to eate,

Would a might eate his last for the love hee beares to

Churchmen.

<u>2</u> <u>Frier</u>

I am of thy minde to, and so it should be and we might be

our owne carvers.   5

I mervaile why they dine heere in the Orchard.

<u>1</u> <u>Frier</u>

I know not, nor I care not. The King coms.

<u>Enter</u> <u>King</u> John, <u>the</u> <u>Bastard,</u> <u>the</u> <u>Abbot,</u> <u>and</u> Thomas <u>the</u>

<u>Monke.</u>

<u>K</u>. <u>John</u>

Come on Lord Abbot, shall we sit together?

<u>Abbot</u>

Pleaseth your Grace sit downe.

<u>K</u>. <u>John</u>

Take your places sirs, no pomp in penury, all beggers   10

and friends may come, where necessitie keepes the house,

curtesie is bard the table, sit downe <u>Phillip</u>.

<u>Bastard</u>

My Lord, I am loth to allude so much to the proverb honors

change maners: a King is a King, though fortune do her

worst, and we as dutifull in despight of her frowne, as 15

if your highnesse were now in the highest type of dignitie.

<u>K</u>. <u>John</u>

Come, no more ado, and you tell me much of dignitie, youle

mar my appetite in a surfet of sorrow.

What cheere Lord Abbot, me thinks you frowne like   IIE2
an host that knowes his guest hath no money to pay   20
the reckning?

Abbot

No my Liege, if I frowne at all, it is for I feare this
cheere too homely to entertaine so mighty a guest as
your Majesty.

Bastard

I thinke rather my Lord Abbot you remember my last   25
being heere, when I went in progresse for powtches--and
the rancor of his heart breakes out in his countenance,
to shew he hath not forgot me.

Abbot

Not so my Lord, you, and the meanest follower of his
majesty, are hartely welcome to me.   30

Thomas

Wassell my Liege, and as a poore Monke may say, welcome
to Swinsted.

K. John

Begin Monke, and report hereafter thou wast taster to a King.

Thomas

As much helth to your highnes, as to my own hart.

K. John

I pledge thee kinde Monke.   35

Thomas

The meriest draught that ever was dronk in England. Am I
not too bold with your Highnesse.

<u>K</u>. <u>John</u>

Not a whit, all friends and fellowes for a time.

<u>Thomas</u>

If the inwards of a Toad be a compound of any proofe: why

so it works.   He <u>dyes</u>.   40

<u>K</u>. <u>John</u>

Stay <u>Phillip</u> wheres the Monke?

<u>Bastard</u>

He is dead my Lord.

<u>K</u>. <u>John</u>

Then drinke not <u>Phillip</u> for a world of wealth.

<u>Bastard</u>

What cheere my Liege, your cullor gins to change.

<u>K</u>. <u>John</u>

So doth my life, O <u>Phillip</u> I am poysond.   45

The Monke, the Devill, the poyson gins to rage,

It will depose my selfe a King from raigne.

<u>Bastard</u>

This Abbot hath an interest in this act.

At all adventures take thou that from me.

There lye the Abbot, Abbey Lubber, Devill.   50

March with the Monke unto the gates of hell.

How fares my Lord?

<u>K</u>. <u>John</u>

<u>Phillip</u> some drinke, oh for the frozen Alps,

To tumble on and coole this inward heate,

That rageth as the fornace sevenfold hote,   55

To burne the holy three in <u>Babylon,</u>   IIE2^V
Power after power forsake their proper power,
Only the hart impugnes with faint resist
The fierce invade of him that conquers Kings,
Help God, O payne, dye <u>John,</u> O plague   60
Inflicted on thee for thy grievous sinnes.
<u>Phillip</u> a chayre, and by and by a grave,
My leggs disdaine the carriage of a King.

<u>Bastard</u>

A good my Lege with patience conquer griefe,
And beare this paine with kingly fortitude.   65

<u>K</u>. <u>John</u>

Me thinks I see a cattalogue of sinne
Wrote by a fiend in Marble characters,
The least enough to loose my part in heaven.
Me thinks the Devill whispers in mine eares
And tels me tis in vayne to hope for grace,   70
I must be damnd for <u>Arthurs</u> sodaine death,
I see I see a thousand thousand men
Come to accuse me for my wrong on earth,

And there is none so mercifull a God

That will forgive the number of my sinnes.   75

How have I livd, but by anothers losse?

What have I lovd but wrack of others weale?

When have I vowd, and not infringd mine oath?

Where have I done a deede deserving well?

How, what, when, and where, have I bestowd a day   80

That tended not to some notorious ill.

My life repleat with rage and tyranie,

Craves little pittie for so strange a death.

Or who will say that <u>John</u> disceasd too soone,

Who will not say he rather livd too long.   85

Dishonor did attaynt me in my life,

And shame attendeth <u>John</u> unto his death.

Why did I scape the fury of the French,

And dyde not by the temper of their swords?

Shamelesse my life, and shamefully it ends,   90

Scornd by my foes, disdained of my friends.

Bastard   IIE3

    Forgive the world and all your earthly foes,

    And call on Christ, who is your latest friend.

K. John

    My tongue doth falter: <u>Philip,</u> I tell thee man,

    Since <u>John</u> did yeeld unto the Priest of <u>Rome,</u>   95

    Nor he nor his have prospred on the earth:

    Curst are his blessings, and his curse is blisse.

    But in the spirit I cry unto my God,

    As did the Kingly Prophet <u>David</u> cry,

    (Whose hands, as mine, with murder were attaint)   100

    I am not he shall buyld the Lord a house,

    Or roote these Locusts from the face of earth:

    But if my dying heart deceave me not,

    From out these loynes shall spring a Kingly braunch

    Whose armes shall reach unto the gates of <u>Rome,</u>   105

    And with his feete treade downe the Strumpets pride,

    That sits upon the chaire of <u>Babylon.</u>

    <u>Philip,</u> my heart strings breake, the poysons flame

    Hath overcome in me weake Natures power,

    And in the faith of Jesu <u>John</u> doth dye.   110

Bastard

    See how he strives for life, unhappy Lord,

    Whose bowells are devided in themselves.

    This is the fruite of Poperie, when true Kings

    Are slaine and shouldred out by Monkes and Friers.

Enter <u>a</u> <u>Messenger</u>.

Messenger

    Please it your Grace, the Barons of the Land,   115

    Which all this while bare armes against the King,

    Conducted by the Legate of the Pope,

    Together with the Prince his Highnes Sonne,

    Doo crave to be admitted to the presence of the King.

Bastard

    Your Sonne my Lord, yong <u>Henry</u> craves to see   120

    Your Majestie, and brings with him beside

    The Barons that revolted from your Grace.--

    O piercing sight, he fumbleth in the mouth,

    His speech doth faile:—lift up your selfe my Lord,

And see the Prince to comfort you in death.   IIE3^V   125

Enter Pandulph, <u>yong</u> Henry, <u>the</u> <u>Barons</u> <u>with</u> <u>daggers</u> <u>in</u>
<u>their</u> <u>hands</u>.

<u>Henry</u>

O let me see my Father ere he dye:

O Unckle were you here, and sufferd him

To be thus poysned by a damned Monke.

Ah he is dead, Father sweete Father speake.

<u>Bastard</u>

His speach doth faile, he hasteth to his end.   130

<u>Pandulph</u>

Lords, give me leave to joy the dying King,

With sight of these his Nobles kneeling here

With daggers in their hands, who offer up

Their lives for ransome of their fowle offence.

Then good my Lord, if you forgive them all,   135

Lift up your hand in token you forgive.

<u>Salisbury</u>

We humbly thanke your royall Majestie,

And vow to fight for <u>England</u> and her King:

And in the sight of <u>John</u> our soveraigne Lord,

In spight of <u>Lewes</u> and the power of <u>Fraunce</u>   140

Who hetherward are marching in all hast,

We crowne yong <u>Henry</u> in his Fathers sted.

Henry

Help, help, he dyes, a Father, looke on me.

Pandulph

K. <u>John</u> farewell: in token of thy faith,

And signe thou dyest the servant of the Lord,   145

Lift up thy hand, that we may witnes here

Thou dyedst the servant of our Saviour Christ.

<u>King</u> John <u>dyes.</u>

Now joy betide thy soule:--what noyse is this?

Enter a Messenger.

Messenger

Help Lords, the Dolphin maketh hetherward

With Ensignes of defiance in the winde,   150

And all our armie standeth at a gaze

Expecting what their Leaders will commaund.

Bastard

Lets arme our selves in yong K. <u>Henries</u> right,

And beate the power of <u>Fraunce</u> to sea againe.   IIE4
Pandulph
    <u>Philip</u> not so, but I will to the Prince,   155
    And bring him face to face to parle with you.
Bastard
    Lord <u>Salsbury,</u> your selfe shall march with me,
    So shall we bring these troubles to an ende.
Henry
    Sweete Unckle, if thou love thy Soveraigne,
    Let not a stone of <u>Swinsted</u> Abbey stand,   160
    But pull the house about the Friers eares:
    For they have kilde my Father and my King.
                    <u>Exeunt, bearing the body of King</u> John.

    Scene xvi
    <u>A parle sounded. Enter</u> Henry, Lewes, Pandulph, Salsbury,
    <u>the Bastard, etc., with the body of King</u> John.
Pandulph
    Lewes of Fraunce, yong <u>Henry Englands</u> King
    Requires to know the reason of the claime
    That thou canst make to any thing of his.
    King <u>John</u> that did offend is dead and gone,
    See where his breathles trunke in presence lyes,   5
    And he as heire apparant to the crowne
    Is now succeeded in his Fathers roome.

Henry

    Lewes, what law of Armes doth lead thee thus,

    To keepe possession of my lawfull right?

    Answere in fine if thou wilt take a peace,   10

    And make surrender of my right againe,

    Or trie thy title with the dint of sword?

    I tell thee Dolphin, Henry feares thee not,

    For now the Barons cleave unto their King,

    And what thou hast in England they did get.   15

Lewes

    Henry of England, now that John is dead,

    That was the chiefest enemie to Fraunce,

    I may the rather be inducde to peace.

    But Salsbury, and you Barons of the Realme,

    This strange revolt agrees not with the oath   20

    That you on Bury Altare lately sware.

Salisbury

    Nor did the oath your Highnes there did take

    Agree with honour of the Prince of Fraunce.

Bastard

    My Lord, what answere make you to the King.

Faith Philip this I say: It bootes not me,   25

Nor any Prince, nor power of Christendome

To seeke to win this Iland Albion,

Unles he have a partie in the Realme.

By treason for to help him in his warres.

The Peeres which were the partie on my side,   30

Are fled from me: then bootes not me to fight,

But on conditions, as mine honour wills,

I am contented to depart the Realme.

enry

On what conditions will your Highnes yeeld?

ewes

That shall we thinke upon by more advice.   35

astard

Then Kings and Princes, let these broils have end,

And at more leasure talke upon the League.

Meane while to Worster let us beare the King,

And there interre his bodie, as beseemes.

But first, in sight of <u>Lewes</u> heire of <u>Fraunce,</u>   40

Lords take the crowne, and set it on his head,

That by succession is our lawfull King.

     <u>They</u> <u>crowne</u> <u>yong</u> Henry.

Thus <u>Englands</u> peace begins in <u>Henryes</u> Raigne,

And bloody warres are closde with happie league.

Let <u>England</u> live but true within it selfe,   45

And all the world can never wrong her State.

<u>Lewes,</u> thou shalt be bravely shipt to <u>France,</u>

For never Frenchman got of English ground

The twentith part that thou hast conquered.

<u>Dolphin</u> thy hand, to <u>Worster</u> we will march,   50

Lords all lay hands to beare your Soveraigne

With obsequies of honor to his grave:

If <u>Englands</u> Peeres and people joyne in one,

Nor Pope, nor <u>Fraunce,</u> nor <u>Spaine</u> can doo them wrong.

     <u>Exeunt,</u> <u>bearing</u> <u>the</u> <u>body</u> <u>of</u> <u>King</u> John.

    FINIS.

TEXTUAL NOTES

Scene i

18. us. Exeunt Pembrooke and Salisbury.] Fleay; us.

65. Exeunt Chattilion and Pembrooke.] Hopk.; Exit Chatt.

65.1-2. Enter . . . Bastard] Munro; Enter the Shrive

72. Fraunce. Exit Salisbury.] Stee.; Fraunce.

200. in.] Q1; in . . . ? ‡Fleay, Munro; it? Hopk.; in Galen. conj. Bul.;
    in [the law]? Ever.

230. thy] Capell, Huntington; thy thy Folger.

245. thou Philip? Sprung] Ever.; thou Philip, sprung

248. proceede] Q2; proeede Capell, Huntington; proeeede Folger.

254. Regis] Fleay; Regius

257. mountaines] Fleay; mountaines,

275. cannot] Capell, Huntington; cann ot Folger.

285. hath] Capell, Huntington; ha h Folger.

317.1 Manent] Bowle; Manet

334. company and alone] and company alone

336. slaunder] Capell, Huntington; fiaunder Folger.

    my] Q2; thy

399. death,] death.

400. contempt,] contempt.

417. Ladie Mother] Q1; Lady-Mother ‡Fleay, Munro, Furn.; lady, mother ‡Hopk., Ever.

Scene ii

74.1-2. Queene, . . . etc.] Fleay, Hopk.; Queene, Bastard, Earles, &c.

110. thy] Q3; the

201. who] Q2; who who

227. knowe.] Q2; knowe?

235. throate. Exeunt.] Fleay; throate.

249.2-3. Towne, . . . walls.] Towne.

261.2. Chattilion] Bowle; Castilean

Scene iii

62.1. Enter Pandulph, a Cardynall] Hopk.; Enter a Cardynall

132. good. . . . followers.] Fleay; good?

158. food. . . . body.] food. Exit.

158.1. Enter Arthur] Hopk.; Arthur

165. unreverent] Q2; unrevent

Scene iv

44. fauzen] Morg.; fanzen

Scene v

0.1-2. and . . . Legate.] Fleay; Cardinall Pandolph legate, and Constance.

35. Exeunt K. Philip and Constance.] Fleay; Exeunt.

Scene vi

0.1-3. Enter . . . following.] Munro; Enter Philip leading a Frier, charging him
to show where the Abbots golde lay.

3. Frier Thomas] Frier

17. Frier Thomas] Frier

24. saying,] Q2; saying.

26. sorie,] Q2; sorie.

27. warme] Q1; warn Fleay, Munro, Furn.

31. Frier Anthony] 2. Frier

37. Frier Anthony] Frier

44. Frier Anthony] Frier

69. Frier Thomas] Frier

80. Frier Thomas] Frier

84-85. Nun. We] Fleay; Nun we

88. Frier Laurence] Bul.; Frier

103. Frier Thomas] Frier

Absolve] Bul.; Absolve

115. Si vis] Q3; sivis

125. stands] Q1; ~ , ± Q2, Q3, Bowle, Stee., Nich., Hazl., Hopk.

hazard] Q1; ~ , Fleay; ~ : Munro, Furn.,; ~ ; Bul., Dom.

148. rest. Come on Sir] Q2; rest come one. Sir

Scene vii

16. one] or

28. me. Exeunt Attendants.] Hopk.; me.

50. Arthur Hubert] Hopk.; Hubert

54. Ah] Hopk.; Arthur Ah

Scene viii

0.1 Essex, Penbrooke] Essex, Salisbury, Penbrooke

16. urgde] Q2; urdge

17. Disdaignd] Q2; Disdaingd

43. anon. Exeunt Lords.] Hopk.; anon.

61. eccho] Folger, Huntington; eccho Capell.

84.1. Nobles and Bishops] Nobles

143. me of a] Fleay; me of me of

144. show. Exit Bastard.] Hopk.; show.

148. ruin] ruines

158. Decide,] Decide

194. live. Exeunt the Bastard and the Prophet.] live.

223. clip] Q2; chip

227. Exeunt Nobles.] Fleay; Exeunt.

279. forward] Q1; froward Fleay, Morl. Hopk.

Scene ix

1. Arthur Now] Hopk.; Now

11.1. wakes] Fleay; was

52. Hubert Right] Bul.; Right

68. then.] Munro; then,

109. Exeunt, bearing Arthurs body.] Hopk.; Exeunt.

Scene x

12. vaunt] Q1; ~ , Q2, Q3, Bowle, Stee., Nich., Hazl., Bul., Dom.

16. noonstead] John MacKinnon Robertson, An Introduction to the Study of the Shakespeare Canon (London: G. Routledge; New York: E. P. Dutton, 1924), p. 402; moonsted

36.1. foes. Enter Hubert.] Fleay; foes.

46. word. Exeunt Hubert and Peter.] Fleay; word.

52. Philip] Fleay; John Philip

63. thirst] Q2; thrirst

107. treason.] Q2; treason?

134. delirant] Bowle; delirunt

155. him.-- Exit Attendant.] Hopk.; him.

214. woorse:] Fleay; woorse

219.1. Enter . . . thee.] Hopk.; What newes with thee. / Enter Messenger.

221. Messenger Please] Hopk.; Please

242. peace. Exeunt.] Fleay; peace.

Scene xi

0.1. Salisbury] Chester

0.2. Bewchampe, with others.] Bewchampe, Clare, with others

11. Eustace] Fleay; Eustace,

26.1 Enter . . . lot.] Hopk.; Hap and hartsease brave Lordings be your lot. /
Enter the Bastard Phillip. &c.

Percy,] Fleay; om. Q1

28. Bastard   Amen] Fleay; Amen

43-44. man / (If any heere)] man, / If any heere

53. wrongs] Q1; wrong's Fleay.

110. Which] Q2; With

151. What] Fleay; Penbrooke   What

152. Messenger   The] Fleay; The

157.1.Bigot, Melun, with] Fleay; Bigot, with

175. le] Nich.; la

188. requite] Folger, Huntington; requite Capell.

197. joy] Q2; joy.

251. Ile] Folger, Huntington; Il Capell.

286. hence.   Exeunt.] Bowle; hence

Scene xii

1. Pandulph   Thus] Bowle; Thus

72. Exeunt Lewes and his followers.] Fleay; Exeunt.

89. pride.   Exeunt.] Hopk.; pride.

89.1-2. Lords, Salisbury and Pembrooke.] Hopk.; Lords.

137. farewell.   He dyes.] Bowle; farewell.

155. Exeunt bearing Meluns body.] Exeunt.

Scene xiii

13.1 where.   Enter the Bastard.] Fleay; where.

83.1. Manet Thomas the Monke.] Munro; Manet the Monke.

98.1. Enter the Abbot unperceived.] Enter the Abbot.

101. Thomas] Monk Q1; Monk [aside]. Munro

Scene xiv

22. Fellow] Hopk.; Lewes   Fellow

29. not] Q2; out

Scene xv

1. 1 Frier] Fleay; Frier

4. 2 Frier] Fleay; Frier

7. 1 Frier] Fleay; Frier

7.1. coms. . . . Monke.] Fleay; coms.

16. highnesse] Q2; hignesse

40. works. He dyes.] Fleay; works.

49. me.] Q1; me: [Stabs him. ±Hopk., Ever.; me! [Kills the Abbot.] Munro.

50. Abbey] Fleay; Abbey,

Devill.] Q1; devil: [Kills the Abbot.] Fleay.

hote,] Bowle; hote.

56. three] Bowle; tree

106. treade] Q3; treads

138. King] Q2; Klng

147. Christ. King John dyes.] Hopk.; Christ.

162. Exeunt, bearing the body of King John.] Exeunt.

Scene xvi

0.1-2. Enter . . . John.] Lewes, Pandulph, Salsbury, &c.

54. wrong. . . . John.] wrong.

EXPLANATORY NOTES

Scene i

2. bereft] removed by violence

8. Emperie] dominion

18. requires] asks

19. Dare lay my hand] I dare wager

21. Nephew] grandson

26. wild] willed, desired

30. guardain] keeping, guardianship. OED notes this spelling as a variant of
guardian, though it records no sense of guardian equivalent to "guardianship."

31. Brittaine] Brittany (disyllabic here and throughout)

55. sticke] hesitate, scruple

62. as we are advisde] since we have received notice

65.1. Shrive] sheriff. "In England before the Norman Conquest . . . a high officer,
the representative of the royal authority in a shire, who presided in the
shire-moot, and was responsible for the administration of the royal desmesne
and the execution of the law. After the Conquest, the office of sheriff
was continued. . . ." (OED)

70. Wil them come] desire (ask) them to come

75. unnaturally] in violation of blood kinship. Cf. x.141.

85. discover] reveal

92. Prince his] prince's

102. too] to

103. Markes] In England, after the Conquest, the value of the mark (a denomination
of weight for gold and silver) was set at two thirds of the pound sterling
(OED).

106. indubitate] undoubted

110. Fond] foolish

138. rented] torn, distracted

143. masserate] cause to waste away

172. presence] assembly

174. rest he] let him remain

181. groome] fellow (contemptuous)

185. teemde] bore offspring

186. cunning] skillful

188. Spit in your hand] prepare for a fresh (and hopefully more successful)
     effort. This sense may be gathered from the examples given in The Oxford
     Dictionary of English Proverbs, 3rd ed., rev. F. P. Wilson (Oxford: Clarendon
     Press, 1970), p. 766, e.g. J. Heywood, A dialogue conteining . . . the
     proverbes in the Englishe tongue, II.iv.G4v: "Naie, I will spyt in my handes,
     and take better holde."

194. lively counterfet] life-like replica

195. Cordelion] Coeur de Lion: lion-heart

196. indifferent] impartial

199. Omne . . . idem] "Things similar are not all identical."

200. Or have read in.] One editor's conjecture is as uncertain as another's;
     parts of two lines may be missing.

208. frivolous] "Law. In pleading: Manifestly insufficient or futile" (OED).

209. chalenge] lay claim to

211. doome] judgment, decision

213. For] because

216. chalenge] accuse

219. loose] lose, suffer loss

223. thrice] This command is not explicitly carried out.

228. aske my felow . . .] A common proverb, according to Tilley, p. 209, who
     quotes an explanation given by James Kelly in A Complete Collection of
     Scotish Proverbs (1721), p. 285: "Spoken when Men appeal for a Character
     to them who are their Associates, or as bad as themselves."

231. Mas] mass. Shortened from by the mass.

     and] if

235. Faith] An asseveration shortened from in faith, or the like.

     you sure] Sure could modify the verb on either side; unpunctuated, it seems
     to refer to both--a freedom with grammar common enough in spontaneous speech.

238. demaund] ask

244. Philippus atavis aedite Regibus] Cf. Horace, Odes, I, i, 1: "Maecenas atavis edite regibus" ("Maecenas, descended from royal ancestors").

246. Quo me rapit tempestas] Horace, Epistles, I, i, 15: "Quo me cumque rapit tempestas" ("Wherever the weather drives me"). Here the meaning is: "Whither does [this] storm carry me?" (cf. 1. 259).

249. hollow] connoting the mystery and ominousness of the supernatural. Cf. Shakespeare, The Tempest, IV.i.138.S.D.; and 1 Henry IV, V.i.1-6.

252. in consort] in company, in accord

254. Records] confirms, attests

Regis] Bullough translates Philippus Regius filius as "Philip, Royal son." But Philippus Regis filius ("Philip [is] a king's son") continues more exactly the set of parallels begun in lines 250 and 252.

257. mountaines] Mountains are not mentioned as a separate element in the series of witnesses which this line summarizes. Perhaps a line or more is missing after 250, but "mountains' echo" seems more obvious.

259. fond] foolish

whether] whither

264. for why] because

265. stoupe] "Of a hawk or other bird of prey: . . . to swoop" (OED).

268. madding vaine] frenzied vanity

272. Speak] state, say

sodaine] sudden, prompt

302. throughly] thoroughly

307. Or . . . name.] The text seems corrupt; perhaps a line or more is missing.

309. checke] restrain, control, (but also) rebuke

mates] The word connotes contempt.

312. ceaze] seize

320. sute] suit, request

321. some money matter] something pertaining to sexual generation. In Shakespeare's Bawdy, 2nd ed. (New York: E. P. Dutton, 1955), Eric Partridge equates purse and scrotum (p. 174), and defines spend as "to expend sexually; to discharge seminally" (p. 191). Lady Margaret's remark may be construed thus: "Like money in a chest, the truth about your generation (you suppose) burns in my bosom." The first lines of the Bastard's reply must be taken either as a deliberate mistaking of her meaning, or as an extension of it.

325. such . . . grant,] such a suit that, if some other might grant it,

327. A] in

332. tilteth] fights, struggles

334. company and alone] I have seen no explanation of the reading in Q1; my emendation makes the whole line a rhetorical chiasmus.

336. my] If thy thoughts in Q1 be construed as "[my] thoughts of thee," the reading is possible, but too awkward to be probable.

337. resolve] inform

342. silly] pitiable (or) insignificant

344. instance] proof, evidence

     extraught] derived, descended

347. close] come to terms

348. affects] feelings

350. remit] forgive, pardon

352. conceipt] notion, idea

358. frame] fashioning

361. challenge] have a natural right to

367. chayre] "A seat for one person (always implying more or less of comfort and ease)" (OED)--here in contrast with the "seate of steele."

369. carpe] OED cites the passage as its only illustration of this definition: "(?) To censure; to judge, discriminate."

373. Nero] Nero was reputed to have murdered his mother.

390. Ist] Is it

396. maind] maimed

403. something] somewhat

405. Romane Dame] Lucrece, whose rape prompted her suicide

407. expostulate] discuss

412. with childe of] pregnant with

413. the rather] the more quickly

415. Robin] familiar or slighting for Robert

417. Ladie Mother] It is not clear which of the two senses suggested by the editors' punctuation is intended.

419. let . . . game] Perhaps "I'll take care of myself." I have found no proper explanation of this expression; but cf. King John, IV.ii.93-95:

> It is apparent foul-play; and 'tis shame
> That greatness should so grossly offer it:
> So thrive it in your game! and so, farewell.

423. Sit fast] Expressing a threat, as in 3 Henry VI, V.ii.3; cf. iii.21.

proudest] most valiant

Scene ii

3. puissant] mighty

4. Cordelions] Richard Coeur de Lion was killed at the siege of Limoges. The play confuses the Duke of Austria with Limoges.

11. unresisted] irresistible

15. impugne] withstand

17. rebate] withdraw

23. rule and almost raigne] OED calls reign "power or rule (of persons) comparable to that of a king."

27. of no esteeme] negligible

34. Yet . . . cause] That is, their valor was taken as a matter of course.

37. reede] counsel, advice

39. trow] believe confidently, feel sure

42. outrovde] outshot (with arrows)

43. lie so long to catch] wait so long in ambush

50. one selfe bottome] the same vessel

52. inferre] report, relate

58. Conjuring] entreating, beseeching

60. state] "Law. The interest which any one has in a property; right or title to property" (OED).

61. studious] solicitous

62. More circumstance the season intercepts] the occasion interrupts a more detailed account

73. Neece] granddaughter

75. Me seemeth] it seems to me

77. Confines] territory

81. discharge] inform

82. list] choose, care, desire

86. begirt] enclose, surround

94. resort] assemblage, gathering

98. inferre] bring forward, adduce

101. overseer] "A person (formerly) appointed by a testator to supervise or assist the executor or executors of the will" (OED).

106. intends] interprets, holds

112. Beshrew] evil befall

    els] otherwise

116. beame] An allusion to Matthew vii.3: "And why seest thou the mote, that is in thy brother's eye, and perceivest not the beame that is in thine owne eye?" (Geneva version, 1560).

117. cousin] "A collateral relative more distant than a brother or sister" (OED).

119. I] aye

122. unnurtred] undisciplined, unchastened

130. case] skin, hide

133. Me thinkes] it seems to me

134. president] precedent

138. choller] choler, anger

    consistorie] standing-place, station

141. straight] straightway, immediately

142. moniment] memento

143. Savages] wild beasts

146. coystrell] knave, base fellow

    swad] bumpkin, lout

148. coverture] garment

149. temper] "To control or restrain oneself" (OED). Perhaps the meaning is: "Scarce can I temper myself, by due obedience, . . . from acting outrage. . . ."

154. review] see again

165. nothing brooke with mee] tolerate me not at all

170. set right in chaunce of warre] make justice depend on the hazard of battle

173. suborned] supported, assisted

182. latest] last

185. yeeld an instance] "Adduce an example in illustration or proof" (OED).

197. false pretended] falsely claimed

205. And] if

209. triall] inquiry

218. intertaine] treat

223. tries] proves, demonstrates

238. Eban] ebon, black, dark

240. Mors] Death

242. temper] concoct

249. statue] Dominic (p. 247) cites Raoul Le Fevre's Recuyell of the Historyes of Troye (written in 1464; translated and published by Caxton in 1471), which recounts that upon the death of Hector the Trojans erected on his tomb "a grete ymage of gold that was maad after the semblance of hector And had the vysage torned toward the grekes and helde a naked swrde [sic] and semed that he manaced the grekes."

260. parle] The meter requires two syllables, as in Hero and Leander, I, 185 and Soliman and Perseda, 1323–1324.

269. wisely] carefully

277. conscience] internal conviction

295. earst] not long ago

312. motion] proposal

315. lustie] valiant, courageous

329. Dolphin] dauphin

359. pheere] fere, consort, spouse

369. affect] fancy, like

371. Swounds] God's wounds (a strong oath)

372. slave] low-born fellow

377. pollicie] political cunning; crafty device, stratagem

    compound] settle

380. front] This word is deliberately ambiguous, meaning (a) confront, and (b) endow his front (forehead) with horns--the fabled fate of the cuckold.

393. I] aye

394. Beldames] aged woman's

400. winke at] disregard, overlook

406. mend] surpass, better

    amplifie] augment

419. sanz] without

438. Now] now that, since

    sorted] come about, turned out

440. presently] at once, directly

441. Presence] assembly, company

444. events] outcomes

450. poyse] weight

454. hap] good fortune, success

460. breath] breathe

462. misbeliefe] atheism (demonstrated in the impudence of breaking an oath made in the name of God)

466. brat] child (contemptuous)

472. thriftles] unthriving, unfortunate

479. stay] obstacle, hindrance

483. moodie] Probably the author meant "muddy" with a play on a figurative sense of the word: "gloomy, sullen" (OED).

486. wrack] adversity, misfortune

Scene iii

17. superficies] surface

21. sit fast] see i.423, and note.

25. words are past] verbal commitments have been given

42. Els] otherwise

56. geere] affair, business

59. forwardnes] eagerness, zeal

66. Sea] see

70. disanull] disallow; annull

79. poling penie] poll-tax

81. temrall] temporal

95. every] every one

101. the Fox] In the proverb curst means "fierce" or "vicious"; John makes a play on the word.

    a] he

120. accompted] accounted, reckoned

183. relyes] OED treats rely in this sense as a different word from rally, and not merely as a spelling variant.

Scene iv

5. gardance] keeping, guardianship

17. and fat of] Either "and with the fat of" or "and fatten off."

20. convert] divert

39. to England] be gone to England

44. fauzen] "Fanzen. I do not know this word. Is it Franciscan? or misprint for fausen, false?" (Fleay). The former seems unlikely; the latter is probable (see vi91 and note), though OED gives fazen as a nineteenth-century dialectical form of fausen, "a kind of eel."

Scene v

0.102. On the entrance and exit of Constance, see the introduction to the text, n.20.

1. attacht] seized, attacked

16. aggravate] add weight to; increase

28. wrack] ruin, destruction

42. conceipt] notion, idea

44. My Father . . . words] it requires your good words to make my father act

46. want] be lacking

Scene vi

3. Benedicamus Domini] Correct Latin for "Praise we the Lord" is Benedicamus
   Domino; here the rhyme prevails.

5. S. Withold] For Saint Withold (evidently unhistorical) as protector, cf.
   Lear, III.iv.120-124:

>   Swithold footed thrice the 'old,
>   He met the night-mare and her nine-fold;
>   Bid her alight,
>   And her troth plight,
>   And aroint thee, witch, aroint thee!

7. S. Charitie] Cf. "E. K." on "Sweete S. Charitie" (Spenser's Shepheardes
   Calender, May, 247): "The Catholiques comen othe, and onely speache, to
   haue charitye alwayes in their mouth, and sometime in their outward Actions,
   but neuer inwardly in fayth and godly zeale" (quoted, in part, by Onions).

9. In nomini Domini] Latin grammar gives way to an internal rhyme; in nomine
   Domini means "in the name of the Lord."

13. conjure ye] Appealing to its "metrical variety" Gary concludes (p. 50)
    that this scene is interpolated. But the macaronics, fourteeners, skeltonics,
    and three-syllable rhymes occur in the monastics' dialogue as instances of
    the verbal rigmarole which Elizabethan protestants associated with Catholicism.
    Cf. Philip's "put you downe with ryming" (vi.16); and the development of
    hocus pocus from words of the Latin mass: hic est corpus--"this is my body."

14. waste] waist

15. Bungie] "Is there any allusion to Friar Bungay?" (Fleay). "The town of
    Bungay in Suffolk . . . once possessed a famous monastery . . ." (Hopkinson).
    "Perhaps from 'bung', a pickpocket" (Bullough). For bungy Halliwell gives
    "intoxicated." But OED offers "? Puffed out, protuberant" for bungy; this
    could allude to the obesity popularly attributed to friars.

17. A] ah. The Latin equivalent follows.

    parce] have mercy

27. warme] "Warn--warrant" (Fleay). I.e., "keep safe, protect." But warn
is corrupted here for another rhyme (cf. vi.3, 9).

29. rabble] "A long string or series of words, etc., having little meaning or
value" (OED).

30. lozell] worthless person

32. Covent] convent

34. by and by] at once

35. and] if

38. wanteth] lacks

48. Sancte benedicite] holy blessing

53. facte] faced

61. Dirige] dirge: Office of the Dead; or Evensong

69. Frier Thomas] Except for the first speech of Friar Laurence the remaining
speeches marked Frier in Q1 could be assigned to Anthony instead; but
Thomas was the original spokesman.

72. Conney] whore

74. presse] "A large (usually shelved) cupboard, esp. one placed in a recess
in the wall" (OED).

75. gis] "Mincing pron[unciation] of Jesus or Jesu" (OED).

77. cotton] prosper, succeed

82. Haud credo Laurentius] Literally, this phrase means "I do not at all believe,
Laurence"; in this context, "Scarcely do I believe, Laurence."

88. Amor vincit omnia] "Love conquers all." "Not Cato, but Virgil, Ecl. X, 69"
(Bullough).

90. mould] earth

92. fausen] Halliwell notes, without a specific citation, that Gower uses the
word to mean "False; bad; sly."

94. passing] surpassingly, very

98. fault my ayme] blame my aim

101. quite] quit, release, redeem

102. Peccavi, parce me] I have sinned, have mercy on me

103. <u>Absolve</u>] The meter requires the trisyllabic Latin imperative singular.

105. for hurting them] "For <u>hurting</u>--instead of whipping" (Fleay).

106. <u>tempus</u> <u>edax</u> <u>rerum</u>] "Time, destructive of [all] things" (Ovid, <u>Metamorphoses</u>, XV, 234).

108. <u>vanitas</u> <u>vanitatis</u>] vanity of vanity. Cf. the first words of Ecclesiastes.

109. <u>aetatis</u>] lifetime

114. <u>Exaudi</u> . . . <u>veniam</u>] Heed me Lord; if thou wilt, have mercy on me. I shall give money, if I have indulgence.

123. reed] read

125. stands in hazard] Editors' changes in punctuation alter the evident meaning of Q1: "The chances are that your destiny is death by falling." "Beware of heights" is a Delphic warning like "beware of water."

127. a] on

149. a Prophets rewarde] Cf. Matthew x.41: "He that receiveth a Prophet in the name of a Prophet, shal receive a Prophetes rewarde" (Geneva version, 1560).

Scene vii

8. adventure] venture, enterprise

9. sodainly] speedily

15. Gramercie] thanks

16. one] Q1 is doubly awkward: it involves a phrase introduced (redundantly) by two prepositions; it makes that phrase do double grammatical duty, modifying <u>known</u> in one clause and <u>is</u> in another. There is no parallel in the play for such a construction.

26. send] grant

27. reave] take away

30. plead the case] This might mean either "explain yourself" (<u>your</u> case), or "assist me" (<u>my</u> case).

41. Tis . . . heare] Two senses are equally possible: (1) "Tis hell, tis horror, tis not fit to be heard"; (2) "Not to be told is hell and horror."

56. venyme] venom

60. triumph] The mood is infinitive: = "to triumph."

64. cyte] summon, arouse

65. knock] "To strike with astonishment, alarm, or confusion" (OED).

69. warrant . . . blisse] surety for your physical saftey

73. exterior] outside part, external

77. Advise thee] consider

91. if thou as they proceede] The sense of the whole construction is "if you proceed as they do, and conclude their judgment with so vile a deed."

105. eyes] heavenly bodies

111. guerdon] reward, requital

127. exempt] excluded: rejected

131. langor] pain. Cf. Hubert's report to John (viii.212-3):

> Nor see nor feele, for of the extreame paine,
> Within one hower gave he up the Ghost.

134. state] office of power (as king)

138. offend] harm, injure

139. issue] enterprise, venture

Scene viii

0.1. Essex, Pembrooke] Salisbury neither speaks nor is heard from in this scene

2. fond] foolish

6. buckling with] engaging

9. trentall] A trental is "a set of thirty requiem masses, said on the same day or on different days" (OED).

10. months minde "The commemoration of a deceased person by the celebration of masses, etc., on a day one month from the date of his death" (OED).

19. earst] formerly, of old

28. Sith] since

proyned] pruned

more than needfull] superfluous

30. resteth] remains (that)

36. censure] judgment, opinion

38. Would] it would

43. anon] straightway, at once

46. cheere] hospitable entertainment

59. fore] before

73. chats] prates, babbles

77. mervailes] marvels

79. had I wist] If I had known; here = the unexpected contingency

83. anon] by and by

86. Admire] feel surprise; wonder

92. in] through, by

111. Please it] if it please

114. past] passed

118. durance] imprisonment

121. thence] "from the prison" (Munro)

124. muse] murmur, complain

140. event] fate

146. prodigious] ominous, portentous

148. ruin] On the reading of Q1, before means "in front of" and the lines must then describe a city already destroyed; but the following lines indicate that the time is before the destruction of Jerusalem: hence "Before (i.e., prior to) the ruin."

158. Decide] determine, demonstrate

     in cyphering] by showing forth, by portraying

169. tempt] risk the perils of

179. for] because

180. private] particular, special

191. suppose] supposition

192. secretarie] confidant

209. extinct] extinguished

223. clip] One does not _chip_ a flower, despite Wilson's suggested parallel
     (p. xxix) from _Euphues_: "a fine face . . . the beautie whereof is parched
     with the Sommers blase, & chipped with the winters blast" (Bond, _Works
     of_ _John_ _Lyly_, I, 202).

233. buggs words] verbal threats. A _bug_ is an object of terror.

234. least] lest

     prevent the issue of] put the outcome beyond

235. corzie] corrosive; grievance

239-240. such luck . . . shame] such griefs are inevitable to one whose
         self-defeating cunning shames the devil

242. frame] contrivance

244. shrowdly] shrewdly, wickedly

     room] position

247. conscience] internal conviction

254. soveraigne types] supreme foreshadowings

255. wherein] The reference is to _types_, not to _discontent_.

276. Bandie] throw aside

279. forward] The emendation of Fleay _et al_. is unneeded. Hubert's hand was
     "froward" after it had been made _weake_ (280), but previously it was "forward."

282. purveyer] supplier, procurer

284. passions] anger

288. storie out] _OED_ quotes this passage as the sole illustration of the
     definition: "? to unravel the true story of."

Preface to Part II

2. Gives period] terminates, concludes

8. returne] turn back

9. parted] departed

12. fond] foolish

14. infancie] youth, minority

Scene ix

3. venter] venture

11.1 wakes] <u>Was</u>, with a participle of motion understood, is possible, but very awkward.

28. pollicie] craftiness

29. undermine] question guilefully

32. closely] secretly

35. a] at

37. ruthfull] lamentable, piteous

44. bootlesse] useless

46. rests] remains

67. condition] mental disposition

70. Maugre] in spite of

72. gave me] granted me to be

82. packet] dispatch

87. bard] barred, forbidden

96. Allyes] kinsmen

97. famous] excellent, magnificent

101. advise] determination, plan

108. letting] preventing

Scene x

8. Prodigies] omens, portents

12. vaunt] The punctuation of Q2 <u>et al</u>. makes separate clauses of this line and the next; in Q1 <u>vaunt</u> evidently has <u>prophecies</u> as its direct object.

16. noonstead] <u>OED</u>: "The station or position of the sun at noon." The whole line may be paraphrased: "To the sun's place at noon in the antipodes."

20. <u>Multa</u> . . . <u>labra</u>] "There's many a slip twixt cup and lip." The Latin version, from Erasmus' <u>Adagia</u>, I.iv.1, is based on an epigram by Palladas in the <u>Greek Anthology</u>, X, 32.

30. beside] out of, away from

55. latest] last

65. little skild] made little difference, mattered little

81. Thinks long] think it long; wait impatiently

85. fained] feigned

90. passionate effects] disturbing outcomes

95. welkin] sky, firmament

116. foredone] exhausted, overcome

134. <u>Quicquid</u> <u>delirant</u> . . . <u>Achivi</u>] "Whatever aberrations their kings indulge,
the Greeks (are the ones who) suffer," Horace's allusion (<u>Epistles</u>, I.ii.14)
to the pride and lust of Agamemnon and Achilles--divisive influences which
caused the Greeks to be defeated by the Trojans in the field.

141. unnaturall] lacking in maternal feeling and behavior

149. <u>Tullyes</u>] Marcus Tullius Cicero (106-43 B.C.), Roman orator

156. bethinke thee] take thought

163. animates] inspires

168. finely] subtly, cunningly

177. confusion] overthrow, destruction

179. oppugne] fight

204. rew] regard with pity

214-215. or . . . Or] either . . . or

216-217. A miserie . . . power] S. K. Heninger writes: "It was generally agreed
[in the renaissance] . . . that the Sun drew up two sorts of evaporations:
(1) the hot and dry 'exhalations,' which provided the source material
for the wide variety of windy and fiery impressions; and (2) the wet
and usually warm 'vapors,' from which developed all moist meteors.
.   .   .   .

In addition to comets, numerous other meteors could be formed by the
kindling of an exhalation in the highest region of Air. Whereas the
comet continued for several days, however, these other fiery impressions
were unstable appearances that seldom persisted for more than an hour.
Each of these fiery meteors was designated by a descriptive name, so
that William Fulke included paragraphs on 'Burned Stoble or Sparcles
of Fire,' 'Torches,' 'Dansyng or Leaping Goates,' 'Burning Candels,'
'Burning Beames and Round Pillers,' 'Burning Speares,' 'Shieldes,
Globes or Bowles,' 'Lampes,' and 'The Pyramidall Pyller Lyke a Spire
or Broched Steeple.' All these fiery impressions were commonly lumped
together under the term 'apparitions'" (<u>A</u> <u>Handbook</u> <u>of</u> <u>Renaissance</u>
<u>Meteorology</u>, Durham, N.C.: Duke University Press, 1960, pp. 38, 91.

233. vulgar sort] common people

Scene xi

0.1. Salisbury] Probably he enters here; he is not named in the opening
speeches as among the conspirators yet to arrive. Since there is no
comment on a return of Chester from exile (cf. xi.47) the direction for
his entry is probably mistaken.

0.2. Bewchampe, with others.] Clare has no part in this scene or anywhere
else, though Q1 marks his entry.

4. mickle] great

11. Eustace Vescy] "Qq erroneously have a comma between the two, for this is
the character's full name" (Dominic).

21. exspect] await

22. gate] gait

26. disease] uneasiness, disquiet

29. travaile] labor

34. conventickle] "A meeting or assembly of a clandestine, irregular, or illegal
character, or considered to have sinister purpose or tendency" (OED).

37. conceipt] faculty of conceiving

38. levell] aim, guess

39. least] lest

45. kindship] kindness

47. inferre] assert (so too in line 61, below)

49. notice] instance, demonstration

53. wrongs] "Has a line dropped out here?" (Fleay). That seems the most plausible
explanation of such an incoherent passage; Fleay's emendation to wrong's
is not much help, for the antecedent of which (almost certainly one or more
persons "now in presence") is lacking. Wrongs is not so likely a subject
for wish as which, so the verb which should be governed by wrongs is probably
wanting also.

70. sprit] sprite, spirit

71. regiment] regime, rule

75. chalenge] claim

76. uncontrouled] undisputed

77. longeth] belongs

113. on] at, to

122. charters] written pardons (for murder, in this case)

143. I] aye

176. wanton] profuse in growth, luxuriant

186. forwardnes] eagerness. The whole idea is: "Thus Fortune effects means
of content as reward for your zeal."

189. Worlds . . . yours] dying possessed of your favor would be the fulfillment
of all that I desire in the world

194. heard] herdsman

195. winking] shutting eyes

237. event] outcome

247. affiance] confidence, assurance

248. smooth] "Use . . . complimentary language" (OED).

251. guerdon] reward

257. least] lest

260. venyme] venom

271. amisse] misdeed

277. bear . . . hand] abuse with false pretences

Scene xii

23. converse] associate, consort

74. alls one] all is the same; it makes no difference

80. prest] enlisted and assembled

103. traine] trap

119. idle] delirious

120. well advisde] having considered well

wotting] knowing

122. discovered] revealed

124. shade] darken

128. your . . . place] the place where you first drew breath

132. said] spoken, made declaration

139. cooling card] "App[arently] a term of some unknown game, applied
     fig[uratively] or punningly to anything that 'cools' a person's passion
     or enthusiasm" (OED).

151. wont] are accustomed

155. confound] destroy

Scene xiii

8. vilde] vile

12. neare the neere] ne'er the near. For near OED gives: "Nearer to one's
    end or purpose." Yet the whole sentence is obscure, for there is no main verb.

17. attaynt] taint, infect; affect

25. agravate] add weight to, magnify

31. scald] assailed (literally, with scaling ladders)

32. rather chose as sacrifice] An odd usage but clear--and hence not necessarily
    a mark of corruption.

41. faine] willing, glad

51. Galloway] a small riding horse

    free] "Of a horse: Ready to go, willing" (OED).

57. Idea] epitome, ideal

76. cates] dainties, delicacies

79. pass] surpass, excel

83. beholding] obliged, indebted

85. contemne] despise, scorn

101. Thomas] If this and subsequent speeches by the Monk were asides (as Munro
     suggests) we would have to suppose that the Abbot did not hear him; on
     the contrary, in his reverie Thomas fails to hear the Abbot.

102. mumpsimus] "stupid muttering" (Dominic). But OED records as the origin of
     the word an anecdote suggesting another meaning: "a traditional custom or
     notion obstinately adhered to however unreasonable it is shown to be."
     I know no good explanation of this usage.

04. dudgeon dagger] "A dagger with a hilt made of 'dudgeon,'" which is
"a kind of wood used by turners, esp[ecially] for handles of knives,
daggers, etc." (OED).

11. for why] because

14. I . . . mercy] I beg your Lordship's pardon

cene xiv

. as] as if

2. Francus] mythical Trojan founder of France; cf. Aeneas as founder of the Roman
people
6. face] countenance, moral support

9. not] Possibly Q1's out is intentional; but the difference in readings amounts
to two letters turned together.

9. earst] on a former occasion

9. magnanimitie] lofty courage

cene xv

. a] he

. to] too

-5. and . . . carvers] if we might choose for ourselves

7. and] if

2. for] because

6. went in progress] made a state journey

9. proof] goodness, effectuality

1. Stay Phillip] Philip, do not begin to drink

9. adventures] chances, hazards. The phrase means "anyway."

take . . . me] Since it is not clear what Philip does to the Abbot, the
editors' directions here and at line 50 are conjectures; line 51 may be
intended figuratively.

6. three] "Of course Shadrach, Meshech, and Abednego" (Fleay). According
to Daniel iii.19-20 (Geneva version, 1560), "Then was Nebuchadnezzar ful
of rage, and the forme of his visage was changed against Shadrach, Meshach,
& Abednego; therefore he charged and commanded that they shulde heate the
fornace at once seven times more then it was wonte to be heat. And he
charged the most valiant men of warre that were in his armie, to binde Shadrach,
Meshach, and Abednego, & to cast them into the hote fyrie fornace."

57. Power after power . . . power] One faculty after another loses its use.

58. impugnes] withstands

   resist] resistance

59. invade] invasion

64. A] ah

86. attaynt] defile

93. latest] last

98. But . . . God] Cf. Romans viii.15-16: "For ye have not received the Spirit of bondage to feare againe; but ye have received the Spirit of adopcion, whereby we crye Abba, Father. The same Spirit beareth witnes with our Spirit, that we are the children of God" (Geneva version, 1560).

99-101. As . . . house] See the introduction to the play, n. 59.

106-107. And . . . Babylon] The scarlet whore and her Babylon (Revelation xvii) were taken by Catholics as figures for imperial Rome, and by Protestants for the Roman Catholic Church itself.

131. joy] gladden

137. We humbly thanke] Evidently John has raised his hand. Cf. 144-148 below.

143. a] ah

152. Expecting] awaiting

Scene xvi

10. in fine] finally

25. bootes] profits, avails

35. advice] consideration

39. as becomes] in fitting fashion

To coincide with the sailing of the Spanish Armada
against England, Pope Sixtus V reaffirmed his predecessors'
sentence against Elizabeth, which the Armada was expected
to implement. The English version of this document is
known to us through a copy at the Bodleian Library, Oxford,
in the form of a single broadside. It is reproduced here
to illustrate something of the religious and political
atmosphere in which The Troublesome Raigne was written.
The type faces of the original are preserved here, but
the typography is modified as in the text of the play
(with one other regular alteration: the substitution of
/w/ for /vv/). Square brackets indicate the position
and approximate extent of hiatuses where the copy is
imperfect.

A Declaration of the Sentence and deposition of Elizabeth,
the usurper and pretensed Quene of Englande.

SIXTUS the fifte, by Gods providence the universal pastor
of Christes flocke, to whome by perpetual and lawful succession, apperteyneth the care and governement of the
Catholike Churche, seinge the pittyfull calametyes which
heresy hath brought into the renoumed cuntryes of Englande
and Irelande, of olde so famouse for vertue, Religion, &
Christian obedience; And how at this present, through the
impietie and perverse governement of Elizabeth the pretensed
Quene, with a fewe her adhearentes, those kingdomes be
brought not onely to a disordered and perillouse state in
them selves, but are become as infected members, contagious
and trublesome to the whole body of Christendome; And not
havinge in those parts the ordinary meanes, which by the
assistance of Christian Princes he hath in other provinces,
to remedy disorders, and kepe in obedience and ecclesiastical
discipline the people, for that Henry the 8. late kinge of
Englande, did of late yeares, by rebellion and revolte from
the See Apostolike, violently seperate him selfe and his
subjects from the communion and societie of the christian
comon welth; And Elizabeth the present usurper, doth con-
tinewe the same, with perturbation and perill of the cuntryes aboute her, shewinge her selfe obstinate and incor-
rigible in such sorte, that without her deprivation and
deposityon there is no hope to reforme those states, nor
kepe Christendome in perfect peace & tranquillety: Therfore

our Holy Father, desyringe as his duty is, to provide present & effectuall remedy, inspired by God for the universall
benefite of his Churche, moved by the pa[ ]iouler affection
which him selfe and many his predecessors have had to these
natyons, And solicited by the Zelous and importunate instance
of sundry the most principall persones of the same, hath
dealt earnestly with divers Princes, and specially with the
mighty and potent <u>Kinge</u> <u>Catholike</u> <u>of</u> <u>Spaine</u>, for the rever-
ence which he beareth to the See Apostolike, for the olde
Amity betwene his house and the Croune of England, for the
specyall love which he hath shewed to the Catholikes of
those places, for the obteyninge of peace and quietnesse in
his cuntryes adjoyninge, for the augmentinge and increase of
the Catholike faith, and finally for the universall benefite
of all Europe; that he will employe those forces which almighty God hath given him, to the deposition of this woman,
and correction of her complices, so wicked and noysome to
the worlde; and to the reformation and pacification of these
kingdomes, whence so greate good, and so manifold publike
commodeties, are like to ensue.

AND to notefy to the world the justice of this acte,
and give full satisfaction to the subjects of those kingdomes
and others whosoever, and finally to manyfest Gods judgements
upon sinne; his Holynes hath thought good, together with the
declaratory sentence of this womans chasticement, to publish
also the causes, which have moved him to procede against her
in this sorte. FIRST for that she is an Heretike, and Schis-

matike, excommunicated by two his Holines predecessors; obstinate in disobedience to God and the See Apostolike; pre-
suminge to take upon her, contrary to nature, reason, and
all lawes both of God and man, supreme jurisdiction and
spirituall auctority over mens soules. SECONDLY for that
she is a Bastard, conceyved and borne by incestuous adultery,
and therfore uncapable of the Kingdome, aswell by the severall
sentences of Clement the 7. and Paule the 3. of blessed
memory, as by the publike declaration of Kinge Henry him
selfe. THIRDLY for usurpinge the Croune without right, havinge
the impediments mentioned, and contrary to the auncyent acorde
made betwene the See Apostolike and the realme of England,
upon reconciliation of the same after the death of S. Thomas
of Canterbury, in the time of Henry the second, that none
might be lawfu[ ] kinge or Quene therof, without the approba-
tion and consent of the supreme Bishopp: which afterward was
renewed by kinge John, and confirmed by ot[ ]e, as a thinge
most beneficiall to the kingdome, at request and instance of
the lordes and Comons of the same. AND FURTHER for that with
sacrilege an[   ]mpiety, she contineweth violating the solemne
Othe made at her coronation, to mainteyne and defende the
auncyent privileges and ecclesiasticall libe[   ]es of the
lande. FOR MANY and grevous injuryes, extorsions, oppres-
sions, and other wronges, done by her, and suffered to be
done against the poore and inn[ ]cent people of both cuntryes.
FOR sturringe up to sedition and rebellion the subjects of
other nations about her, against their lawfull and naturall

prin[　]s, to the destructyon of infinite soules, overthrow
and desolation of most goodly cittyes and cuntryes. FOR
harboringe and protectinge Heretikes, fugeti[　], rebelles,
and notorious malefactors, with greate injury and prejudice
of divers comon wealthes: and procuringe for the oppression
of Christendome an[　　　]nce of comon peace, to bringe
in our potent and cruell enemy the Turke. FOR so longe and
barbarouse per[　　]on of gods saints, aflictinge,
spolyng[　]al[　]pris[　]ninge the sacred Bishops, torment-
inge, and pittyfully murtheringe numbers of holy Preists,
and other cath[　]like persons. FOR the unnat[　]ral

[　　]ust imprisonment, and late cruelty used against the
most gracyous Princesse, Mary Quene of Scotland, who und[　]r
p[　]omise and assurance of protection a[]d s[　　　]e
first [　]nto Englande. FOR abolishinge the trew Catholike
religion; prophaninge holy Sacraments, Monaste[　]es,
Churches, Sacred [　　　　] Mem[　　　　　　　]w[　]
els so ever migh[　] helpe or further to eternal [　]lvation:
And in the Comonwelth, disgracei[　　　　　]t Nobility,
erecting base and un[　　　　] persons to all the Civile
and Ecclesiastical Dignetyes, sellinge of lawes and justice,
And finally ex[　]ysi[　　　　　]yrannie, with high
offence to [　　]hty God, oppressyon of the people, perdi-
tion of soules, and ruine of those cuntryes.

WHERFORE, th[　　　]ges beinge of such nature & qualety, that some of them make her unable to reigne, others
declare her unworthy [　]o live; His Holinesse, in the al-

mighty pow[   ]d[ ], and by Apostolical auctority to
him committed, doth renewe the sentence of his predecesso[ ]s
Pius 5. and Gregorie the 13. tooching the Excommunication
[   ]position of the sad Elizabeth: and further a newe
doth Excommunicate, and deprive her of all auctority and
P[   ]gnety and of all title and pretensyon to t[   ]
said Croune and Kingdomes of England and Ireland; declaringe
her to be illegittimate, and an unjust usurper o[ ] the
sam[ ], And absolvinge the people of those st[ ]tes, and
other persons whatsoever, from all Obedience, Othe, and other
bande of Su[ ]jection unto her, or to an[ ]other in her
name. And further doth straitely commaunde, under the indig-
nation of almighty God, and payne of Excommunication, and
the corporal punishment appoynted by the lawes, that none,
of whats[ ]ever condition or estate, after notice of these
presents, presume to yeilde unto her, Obedience, favor, or
other succ[ ]re; But that they and every of them concurre by
all meanes possible to her chastisement. To the ende, that
she which so many wayes hath forsaken God and his Churche,
beinge now destitute of wordly comforte, and abandoned of
all, may acknowledge her offence, and humbly submitt her
selfe to the judgements of the highest.

BE IT THERFORE notefyed to the inhabitants of the said
Cuntryes, and to all other persons, that they observe dili-
gently the premisses, withdrawinge all succor publike and
private, from the party pursued and her adherents, after
they shall have knowlege of this present: And that forthwith

they unite them selfs to the Catholike army conducted by the most noble and victorious Prince, <u>Alexander Farnesius</u>, <u>Duke of Parma</u> <u>and</u> <u>Placentia</u>, in name of his Majesty, with the forces that eche one can procure, to helpe and concurre as ys aforesaid (yf nede shall be) to the deposition and chasticement of the said persons, and restitution of the holy Catholike faith. <u>Signifyenge</u> to those which shall doe the contrary or refuse to doe this here commaunded, that they shall not escape condigne punishment.

MOREOVER BE IT KNOWEN that the intention of his Holynesse, of the Kinge Catholike, and the Duke his highnesse in this enterprise, ys not to invade and conquere these kingdomes; chaunge lawes, previleges or customes; bereave of liberty or livelyhoode, and man (other then rebels and ostinate persons) or make mutation in any thinge, except suche, as by comon accorde, betwene his Holinesse, his Catholike majesty, and the states of the lande, shalbe thought necessary, for the restitution and continuance of the Catholike Religion, and punishment of the usurper and her adhearents. <u>Assuringe</u> all men, that the controversyes which may arise by the deprivation of this woman, or upon other cause, eyther betwene particuler partyes, or touching the successyon to the Croune, or betwene the Churche and Comon welthe, or in other wise whatsoever, shalbe decyded and determined wholy accordinge to justice and Christian equity without injury or prejudice to any person. AND there shall not onely due care be had, to save from spoyle the

Catholikes of these cuntryes, which have so longe endured,
but mercy also shewed to such penytent persons, as submitt
them selves to the Capitane generall of this army. Yea for
so much as information ys given, that there be many, which
onely of ignorance or feare be fallen from the fayth, and
yet notwithstandinge are taken for heretikes; Neyther ys
yt purposed, presently to punish any such persons, but to
supporte them with clemency, till by conference with lerned
men and better consideration, they may be informed of the
truth, if they doe not shew them selves obstinate.

TO PREVENT also the sheadinge of Christiane bloode,
and spoyle of the cuntry, which might ensewe by the resistance of some principall offenders. Be it knowne by these
presents, that it shal not onely be lawfull for any person
publike or private (over and besides those which have under-
taken the enterprise) to areste, put in holde, and deliver
up unto the Catholike parte, the said usurper, or any of her
complices; But also holden for very good service and most
highly rewarded, accordinge to the qualety and condition of
the partyes so delivered. And in like maner, all others,
which here to fore have assisted, or herafter shall helpe
and concurr to the punishment of the offenders, and to the
establishment of Catholike Religion in these provinces,
shall receyve that advauncement of honor and estate which
their good and faithful service to the comon welthe shall
require; in which, respecte shalbe used, to preserve the
auncyent and honorable famelyes of the lande, in as much as

ys possible. AND finally by these presents, fre passage ys
graunted to such as wil resorte to the catholike campe, to
bringe victuals, munytion, or other necessaryes; promisinge
liberall payment for all such things, as shalbe received
from them for service of the army. Exhorting withall and
straitely commaunding, that al men accordinge to theire
force and ability, be redy and diligent to assiste here in;
to the ende no occasion be given to use violence, or to
punish such persons as shall neglect this commaundement.

Our said holy father, of his benignety, and favor to
this enterprice, out of the spirituall treasures of the
Churche, committed to his custody and dispensation,
graunteth most liberally, to al such as assist, concurr, or
helpe in any wise, to the deposition and punishment of the
abovenamed persons, and to the reformation of these two
Cuntryes, Plenary Indulgence and perdon of all their sinnes,
beinge duely penitent, contrite, and confessed, according to
the law of God, and usual custome of Christian people.

Laus Deo.